Theory is one thing, practice another. While sketching out Pope Francis's hope and dream that we all become missionary disciples, Deacon John Lozano describes the ways and means of doing this in a practical, pastoral, and challenging fashion. A revolutionary guidebook here! ⇥ **BISHOP ROBERT F. MORNEAU**, *Green Bay, Wisconsin*

146 5569

Most Catholics don't really think of themselves as disciples—but that is just what Jesus calls us to be. Deacon John Lozano's fine book reminds us all how deeply Jesus loves us and desires us to experience how this love can transform our lives. Engaging stories from his pastoral ministry are full of practical wisdom for developing a deeper, more nourishing prayer life, and for growing in a real, adult relationship of love and service with Christ.
⇥ **FR. JOHN RANDALL SACHS, SJ**, *Associate Professor, Boston College School of Theology & Ministry, author of **The Christian Vision of Humanity***

This is one of those rare books that is both inspired and accessible. *Becoming a Fervent Disciple* is a true gift for anyone looking to grow their relationship with God and help others in their community to do the same. ⇥ **MATTHEW F. MANION**, *Faculty Director, Villanova University School of Business Center for Church Management, Former President and CEO, Catholic Leadership Institute*

We live in an age of distraction and discontent. John Lozano's *Becoming a Fervent Disciple* is a summons to turn our hearts to the "one thing necessary." Writing with honesty and wisdom, Lozano offers a practical path to stir into flame our hearts' true desire. The future of the church will be shaped by the intentional choices of fervent disciples. John Lozano equips us for that future.
⇥ **KEVIN L. HUGHES**, *author and Chair of the Humanities Department and Associate Professor of Theology/Religious Studies, Villanova University*

BECOMING A
FERVENT
DISCIPLE

Practical Tools for Developing
a Deeper, Daily Relationship
with Jesus

JOHN P. LOZANO

**TWENTY-THIRD
PUBLICATIONS**
twentythirdpublications.com

For my children:
Hope Marie, John Francis,
and Michael.

For the grace and joy
I knew not possible.

TWENTY-THIRD PUBLICATIONS
One Montauk Avenue, Suite 200
New London, CT 06320
(860) 437-3012 or (800) 321-0411
www.twentythirdpublications.com

Cover photo: © Shutterstock.com / Michaelstockfoto

ISBN: 978-1-62785-341-5
Library of Congress Control Number: 2017958807
Printed in the U.S.A.

 A division of Bayard, Inc.

Contents

WE ARE REVOLUTIONARIES

and, what is more, revolutionaries of this
revolution. For we have taken this road of
the greatest metamorphosis in humanity's
history. In this day and age, unless Christians
are revolutionaries, they are not Christians.
They must be revolutionaries through Grace!
Grace itself. POPE FRANCIS, *The Church of Mercy*

What is a "fervent disciple"?

We often hear phrases like "fervent disciples," "encountering Jesus," and "fervent discipleship" when talking about our commitment to put the words of the gospel into action in our lives. The problem is: What do these phrases really mean? Pope Francis is not bashful with these words. The first sentence of his first apostolic exhortation begins: "The joy of the gospel fills the hearts and lives of all who encounter Jesus."

The focus of this book is to help people of faith identify, understand, and connect their faith experience with these central gospel words and to bring them into their lives as the guiding principle, direction, and goal. Many of us have heard the call to personally encounter Jesus and to develop a personal relationship with God, but very little has been offered on how to make this happen.

This book is an invitation to discover practical ways to make this connection in your life each day, offering suggestions to help you begin a journey of reflection on your life experience and to consider a path that incorporates tools to move all of us toward a dynamic, sustainable, and ever-growing encounter with Jesus and the life of fervent discipleship. This journey and discovery of these tools is for every one of us. In the words of Pope Francis: "No one should think that this invitation is not meant for him or her, since 'no one is excluded from the joy brought by the Lord.'"

CHAPTER ONE

GOOD IS NOT GREAT

Those who are on fire cannot sit in a chair.

I love to watch my son, an experienced camper, build a fire in the woods. He carefully selects certain types of wood that are more ignitable than others and best for the early burning rather than latter fuel for an already blazing fire. He chooses various sizes of wood that he positions with each aligned to the other, forming a strategic structure to create maximum air flow. Most impressively, he is able to ignite the fire with a single match. It is the same in our lives of faith. Once the right pieces are gathered and the pattern is set we are disposed for that single flame of divine love to catch us on fire. Faith has always been about fire.

> Did anything so great ever happen before? Was it ever heard of? Did a people ever hear the voice of God speaking from the midst of fire, as you did, and live? DEUTERONOMY 4:32–33

It is the fire of God's love that sent his Son among us, a revelation of the very heart of God like nothing else in the history of humanity. There is nothing tame, domesticated, or dull in this story; it is a story of fire, and his name is Jesus.

Likewise, there is nothing tame in the life and the words of John the Baptist. "Even now the ax lies at the root of the trees" (Matthew 3:10). "He will baptize you with the Holy Spirit and fire" (Matthew 3:11). And there is nothing tame in the life and the words of Jesus himself:

> "This is the time of fulfillment. The kingdom of God is at hand. Repent, and believe in the gospel." MARK 1:15

> "I have come to set the earth on fire, and how I wish it were already blazing!" LUKE 12:49

These are not the words of a domesticated, provincial Christianity. *These are words of revolution.*

The revolution in these words is unique in that it is not a change of economics or politics but more simply, and more significantly, a change of the human heart. Only God's love can do this, and God accomplishes this through those of us who are fervent followers of the risen Jesus.

Christianity has only one message: that all of humanity come to know and experience the risen Jesus in their lives. From this encounter the human heart is transformed and the gift of eternal life begins.

In the book *Good to Great*, Jim Collins reveals the results of research to answer a fundamental question about business: Why are some companies just "good," while others make the leap to being "great"? He summarizes his findings:

> Good is the enemy of the best. And that is the key reason why we have so little that becomes great. We don't have great schools, principally because we have good schools.....Few people attain great lives, in large part because it is just so easy to settle for a good life. The vast majority of companies never become great, precisely because the vast majority become quite good—and that is their main problem.

When reading these words, I could not help but think about the Christian church. Most churches are good and the faith lives for the vast majority of the followers of Jesus are good, or at least good enough. As a result, we don't strive for the great. Satisfied with being good, our churches play it safe, keeping everything under control and not rocking the boat. We become complacent, more interested in maintenance than we are in mission, because what we currently have is good. When things are good, we just keep going along; we settle; we are tame.

As Jim Collins asks: "Is the disease of 'just being good' incurable?" Jim's answer, and the gospel's answer, is a resounding "NO!" The gospel calls us to be *"on fire"* and members of a revolution. The gospel reveals how this happens: *by personally encountering the risen Jesus and becoming fervent disciples.*

⌇⏐⌇

PERSONAL REFLECTION

How does Collins' observation that "Good is the enemy of the best" speak to your life?

CHAPTER TWO

BORING?

"Nobody ever yawns in the presence of Christ."

SHERRY WEDDELL, *FORMING INTENTIONAL DISCIPLES*

Compared to popular culture and its need to grab our attention at every possible moment, many people might say that Christianity is boring, or at least dull and irrelevant to daily life. And based on the typical experience of church for most people, they're right!

How can this be? While Christianity is not entertainment or about making us feel good about ourselves, the basic message of the Christian faith—how the divine, saving love of the God of the cosmos is given to all humanity in and through his Son, Jesus—is so extraordinary that anyone who hears this message in its fullness with an open mind would be hard pressed to call it dull or irrelevant. Some might question whether or not it is true, but they certainly couldn't call it boring.

It is not the Christian message itself that is the problem but the contemporary experience of Christianity. If this were not the case then Christianity would be thriving when in fact it is not.

TOTAL U.S. CHURCHES	325,000
GROWING U.S. CHURCHES	15,000
% OF GROWING U.S. CHURCHES	5%

For every one person who enters the Catholic Church, more than six Catholics leave.

Anyone passionate about the good news of Jesus Christ should be deeply concerned about this, just as any CEO would be if their company started losing customers at the same rate. I can imagine that CEO calling an emergency meeting of all senior staff to discover the cause of such a dramatic decline and to create ways to reverse it. I can imagine the CEO saying to his senior staff, "We are not leaving this room 'til we figure out how to reverse this trend!" But the most alarming aspect of this decline in the church is that there is no "alarm." If the leaders are not visibly alarmed, then it follows that individual Christians are not alarmed either.

Jesus, the saints, and all passionate followers of Christ through the ages got what was at stake. They got the extraordinary good news of the gospel message of Jesus. In Mark's gospel, the earliest written gospel, the very first words of Jesus illustrate his concern: "This is the time of fulfillment. The kingdom of God is at hand. Repent, and believe in the gospel" (1:15). The "time" Jesus speaks of is the Greek word *kairos*, which means the time filled with meaning and of supreme importance, a time not to be missed. The kingdom of God is now at hand; not just very close or nearby, but here. There is an exigency, an immediacy in Jesus' cry. Often our image of Jesus has been one of him sitting in the field with sheep, calm and collected, not in any hurry, almost without emotion. That is not the Jesus of the Bible.

I think Pope Francis has this same urgency and passion of Jesus when he writes on the very first page of *The Joy of the Gospel*:

> I invite all Christians, everywhere, at this very moment, to a renewed personal encounter with Jesus Christ, or at least an openness to letting him encounter them; I ask all of you to do this unfailingly each day. No one should think that this invitation is not meant for him or her, since "no one is excluded from the joy brought by the Lord." The Lord does not disappoint those who take this risk; whenever we take a step towards Jesus, we come to realize that he is already there, waiting for us with open arms. Now is the time to say to Jesus: "Lord, I have let myself be deceived; in a thousand ways I have shunned your love, yet here I am once more, to renew my covenant with you. I need you. Save me once again, Lord, take me once more into your redeeming embrace.

The words Pope Francis uses here are reminiscent of those first words of Jesus in Mark's gospel. The pope has a clear sense that Christians are just not "getting it." They are not living in a daily personal encounter with the merciful love of God that is transformative and brings us divine joy. This redeeming embrace the pope speaks of is the kingdom of God that Jesus said is "at hand," an intimate encounter with the love of Jesus' Father in and through an encounter with Jesus himself in a personal and life-changing way. This is not a one-time event but a daily encounter that is meant for us all, with no one excluded. To miss this is to miss everything!

*Is it the message of Jesus Christ that is boring
or is it the messengers?*
I went to a Catholic, all boys' high school run by a Franciscan order of priests and brothers. One day we had a "vocations awareness" day. A Franciscan priest came to talk to us about considering the vocation of becoming a religious priest or brother, preferably Franciscan, of course. The priest that came to our school that day gave us a vocations presentation during which he never smiled. In fact, his face looked a bit sour and slightly depressed. Even at eighteen years old I could see something wrong with this picture. I thought to myself, "Here is this priest asking us to consider becoming a religious priest or brother, to embrace poverty, chastity (no small thing when you are an eighteen-year-old male), and obedience, and he is not even smiling?" Being the audacious young adolescent that I was at the time, I went up to this priest after his presentation and said to him. "Father, you never smiled during your presentation to us." The priest replied; "I don't have a good smile." Even at eighteen I knew that was not the reason!

Dullness, not doubt, is the greatest enemy of faith
Skepticism and the questioning of religious faith in general, and Christianity in particular, have always been with us. Doubt in and of itself is not the problem; in fact, doubt is part of every believer's life and can spur on a search and quest for God that deepens our faith. The true problem is a growing lack of fervency within Christianity itself. It has been said Christian faith is "caught" more than it is "taught." The inspiration to live a Christian life comes most often from an encounter with people of faith, a vibrant faith in which the seeking person perceives something new, different,

and attractive in the life of the believer. This has been my own experience as well.

I attended church every Sunday until my teens, and then less frequently. I was not engaged with my faith at all. I still had faith, but God, church, and prayer were on the outskirts of my life. A few months after I turned sixteen, my father died. It was the turning point of my life. What was on the outskirts of my life was suddenly at the center. I found myself asking questions of faith with a seriousness and passion that most sixteen-year-olds do not possess. At my father's funeral, I prayed with an intensity I had never before experienced. I was scared. I prayed for help. All I can say is that day I experienced a presence with me in that church that was real and almost tangible. I had the inner sense that everything would be okay and that I could trust God with my life. Faith began to stir within me that day, and I grew in prayer, trust, and faith in God.

About a year later I was invited to attend a prayer meeting. "A what?" I thought to myself. Then I said, "Whatever! I want to grow closer to God, so I'll check it out." Still a skeptic, I remember going to the prayer meeting and thinking to myself: "It's Friday night. What are these people doing in a church on Friday? It isn't even Sunday!" I noticed that the age range of the people gathered was sixteen to sixty-five. Again I wondered: "Why are all these people of different ages coming together? This is odd." At the same time, I was greeted with a sincere warmth and joy by these people. As I looked into their eyes I saw something. It is hard to describe what that was, but it was something very attractive and compelling. I remember saying to myself, "I don't know what that is they have, but whatever it is, I want it." As the prayer began I did something very simple. I sat down and prayed. Silently, I prayed to God and asked for "whatever *that* is." I remember my time of prayer became filled with what I later discovered are called the fruits of the Holy Spirit: God's love, joy, and peace. It was a compelling and transformative experience.

Fruits of the Holy Spirit (Galatians 5:22)
Love | Joy | Peace | Patience | Kindness | Generosity
Faithfulness | Gentleness | Self-Control

When I look back on my own conversion and faith development, I see that the two elements that disposed me to faith are the two most common experiences in people's lives that prepare them for Christian faith: human suffering and the encounter with people who have vibrant faith. The former is probably the most common for people, and the suffering and deep struggle I experienced at my father's death were the catalyst that brought me to a new openness to God and God's living presence in my life. However, the second trigger for my faith development was equally important and is often overlooked as a primary way that God reaches out to us. It was this encounter with people of vibrant faith that drew me, lured me, and caught my attention to consider in a profoundly new dimension this risen Jesus and the person of the Holy Spirit.

The grace that comes to us through people of vibrant faith is more common than we may realize. It is obvious when we encounter the charismatic preacher, teacher, writer, and social activist. All too often, however, we don't recognize how common the presence of God's grace is among so-called ordinary people. For over forty years I have asked people what they identify as the source of their Christian faith. Often the reply is the influence of a relative like a grandmother or grandfather whose quiet, unassuming life of faith spoke volumes. Or they might mention the experience of accompanying someone through a particularly difficult period of their life, such as a serious illness or crisis, who is able to face that hardship with resilience, peace, and trust in God. We should never sell short the power of Christian witness even when that witness is almost unintentional. This is the power of the person of vibrant faith—what Paul calls a "perfume." What a beautiful image, a scent that draws, lures, captures the attention of the other.

PERSONAL REFLECTION

How have suffering and struggle helped
you become more disposed to faith?

How has the witness of people of vibrant faith
helped you become more disposed to faith?

CHAPTER THREE

FERVENCY

*The continuous course of history requires an endless stream
of new apostles to announce the Gospel and live in the heart
of temporal life like yeast in dough. The new apostles will be
Fervent Disciples of Jesus Christ completely integrated into
their own times. They will be Christians deeply engaged in
the apostolic movement that is best suited to their social and
professional status. In all cases they represent a treasure for
the unity of the Church and her mission.* ST. JOHN PAUL II

Alive

How, then, can we describe fervency, and what are the qualities
that characterize it? To start, fervent disciples are *alive*, engaging
life in a dynamic and spiritual fashion. They approach life with
the clear and express intent to experience it, affect it, and improve
it. This is in contrast to those who live their lives passively, who
are simply along for the ride without any real purpose or drive.

An example of this was a conversation I had with a successful
businessman who had recently experienced a conversion in his

life and was now active in his church and alive in his faith. I asked him to tell me about his conversion experience and he put it this way: "I was converted from complacency." I was struck by his expression. He seemed like a decent enough person, but he said that before his conversion, while he was comfortable and financially successful, his heart and soul were filled with complacency. I think for most people this is what is most challenging: complacency, or worse yet, apathy. Apathy and dullness to the world around us are the greatest enemies of faith. Fervency is meant to be the norm for the Christian disciple. Thomas Merton states this clearly: "All people can seek and find this intimate awareness and awakening which is a gift of love and a vivifying touch of creative and redemptive power, that power which raised Christ from the dead" (*The Hidden Ground of Love*, p. 159).

Jesus' words are very strong and uncompromising on this when he says, "Leave the dead to bury their dead" (Matthew 8:22). In this perspective, hell begins in this life, as the destruction of the soul or the whole personality of a person. What the Book of Revelation calls the "second death" (2:11; 20:6, 14; 21:8)—in this sense, some people are already dead.

Awake-alert

A fervent disciple is awake and alert to the person of Jesus in their life and more importantly to his coming into their lives No one communicates this more than John the Baptist, "The voice of one crying out in the desert: 'Prepare the way of the Lord, make straight his paths.'" The image the Baptist puts forth is that of a person fully engaged, vigilant, and focused in a radical and all-encompassing fashion. This greatest of the prophets reveals a compelling and clarion call toward this disposition of a fervent disciple.

The parable of the wise and foolish virgins in Matthew 25 illustrates this kind of preparedness and readiness for someone who is coming. The wise virgins brought flasks of oil with their lamps as a sign of their conviction that the bridegroom would indeed come and when he came they had what they needed to welcome him. They are an image of a disciple who is alert and actively waiting for a "person" they *expect* to come.

A fervent disciple's heart and mind are set on someone who is himself alive, active, and *coming* to them in their lives. This is a serious story that Jesus tells. It speaks of the utter centrality of this kind of discipleship, since these are the ones who enter the wedding feast (the primary biblical image for our life with God here and in heaven), and those un-fervent disciples are shut out from the feast. In this Scripture passage we see that being a fervent disciple is not an option; fervency is not just for some of us who are more disposed to this sort of thing.

Imagine going through your day seriously focused and attentive to Jesus coming to you in your daily experience. Even the ordinariness of life takes on a unique quality, since one is never outside of the person of the risen Christ.

Direction - life eternal with God thru Jesus

Fervent disciples are going somewhere; they are caught up with a direction and a person other and bigger than themselves.

An example of direction in the life of a fervent disciple is my good friend Ed. Ed is outgoing, funny, and a bit gregarious. Often when he is serving in some form in our church community you will hear him utter to himself, but just loud enough for those around him to hear, "I'm just trying to get into heaven, just trying to get into heaven." When I hear this I smile, knowing he is only half joking. I know Ed is not trying to earn salvation through good works; nor does Ed fear God as one he needs to appease. But I also realize that Ed knows the direction of all his efforts: life eternal with God though Jesus Christ. Ed's little statement is a reminder to him and to all of us of our direction, where all of life is ultimately going, and this makes all the difference in how we go about living each day of our lives. It is why we do what we do.

There is a maxim that says to "begin all things with the end in mind." The fervent disciple not only begins all things with the end in mind, he or she *lives* all things with the end in mind. St. Ignatius of Loyola, founder of the Society of Jesus (the Jesuits), wrote the following passage that I highly recommend you read and ponder slowly. Living these words would be transformative in the life of a disciple:

> For this it is necessary to make ourselves indifferent to all created things…so that, on our part, we want not health rather than sickness, riches rather than poverty, honor rather than dishonor, long rather than short life, and so in all the rest; desiring and choosing only what is most conducive for us to the end for which we are created.

I first read these words of Ignatius during an eight-day Ignatian retreat when my retreat director, Fr. Joe, gave them to me to reflect on. The first day I met Fr. Joe, I noticed he walked with a limp, and I asked him if he had a back problem. Fr. Joe replied, "No, I have a brain tumor." I was stunned. Fr. Joe was a young man, still in his thirties, who had recently finished his PhD in theology and had just received a full-time tenured teaching position at Boston College. I quickly realized that Fr. Joe had finally arrived at the place that he had spent his entire life preparing for—to become a Jesuit, priest, finish his PhD, obtain a teaching position—and just when this all had come together he discovered he had an inoperable brain tumor. My eight days on retreat with Fr. Joe were extraordinary. Fr. Joe did not want to die, and he asked me and many others to pray for his healing. He also said he had some very hard days. At the same time, I saw a man before me who had accepted his illness and continued his ministry, his discipleship, by doing the work he was physically able to do: spiritual direction. Joe remained deeply prayerful and full of faith and exhibited a pleasant joyfulness and profound gentleness. He was at peace. I knew as I read these words of Ignatius that I was before a man who lived them. There is an extraordinary freedom that comes with being a fervent disciple. A freedom even death cannot take from us.

"Indifference" does not mean we do not care; it means we care very deeply but about the right things. For the fervent disciple, it is all about the direction and ultimate end of life: life with Jesus Christ, our goal and our love. Everything is relativized in light of this end and in consideration of our love for this person, Jesus. This does not lead to a rejection of the goodness in this world or a lack of participation in the affairs of human life. Quite the opposite. Once our focus and direction are clear, everything in life finds its fulfillment and beauty.

Intentionality

Once a person of faith has the direction of a disciple of Jesus, then his or her choices in life become intentional, reflecting and forwarding the direction and goal of their life. There is now a reason to pray, to go to church, to serve the poor, to grow closer to the person of Jesus.

I intentionally choose to pray daily, to read and develop my understanding of my faith. I make thoughtful and intentional choices about the people I will develop as friends and what activities in life I will engage in. Intentional disciples simply do not go with the flow of the culture around them. Intentional disciples are always asking themselves questions like: "How will this person, this activity, this commitment, affect my life, and how will it help or hinder my goal to be a disciple of Jesus?"

For example, a fervent disciple of Jesus would not take a job in a different part of the country without first considering how it would affect his or her faith life, vocation as spouse and parent, and the health and faith development of his or her family. A fervent disciple would be hard pressed to leave a vibrant faith community, and would not just consider the bigger paycheck or career advantage. Intentional disciples think about life in this way.

Consider my friend Michael. When he started college, he looked around at his peers and saw how those who came to college with faith and commitment to the church community soon found themselves in an environment that did not support and even worked against these commitments. Michael observed the ethical and religious struggles of his classmates and noticed how quickly their faith and morals took a back seat to the new social environment of college, and he didn't want that to happen to him. What Michael decided to do early on in his time at college was to come to our campus ministry office and seek the kind of support he knew he needed to achieve the goal that was important to him—continuing and strengthening his faith in Jesus and his relationship with the church community. Michael and I worked together, and he became very involved in our ministry; he flourished as a person of faith during his college years. Michael went on to serve in various ministries in the church. He often looks back on his college years as particularly formative in his life and future ministry—a ministry that was made possible by the decisions of an intentional, fervent disciple. Fervent disciples are not people who just go with what is popular at the time and allow their environment and people they associate with to determine their choices and the direction of their lives. They "do all things with the end in mind." Their goal is to follow Jesus Christ and to live with him in eternity, and they do the things that will help them continue on their path and achieve that goal.

What fervency is not

Let us look at what fervency is not. Fervency is not primarily an emotion. Therefore, fervency cannot be dismissed by thinking, "I'm not a very emotional person, so fervency is not for me." Fervency is also not a certain personality type. We have all met people of deep, fervent faith who possess very different personalities. One can be quiet, unassuming, and introverted while another is talkative, socially engaging, and extroverted. Both can be fervent disciples! Fervency is not primarily about excitement and enthusiasm; nor is it essentially about discovering your passions, talents, or gifts. Let us also be clear that these are all-important elements of the fervent life of faith, but they are not the primary source.

Fervency is also not something that happens only when everything is going well and all the conducive conditions for a fervent life of faith are present, such as being inspired by a recent homily, talk, or book; having had a really good conversation with another person of faith; having positive relationships with all the people in your life; and good health and feeling close to God in prayer or in church. Fervent disciples are not people who never have a bad day, never feel down, never get cranky, never feel distant from God, and never go through a "dark night" of the soul in their journey of faith. One need only look at the lives of the saints, the most fervent disciples, to see people who have struggled with all of the above, especially with long periods of spiritual dryness. The words of Thérèse of Lisieux are chilling when she speaks of her trial of faith as a "night of nothingness" (*Story of a Soul*). The revelations of St. Teresa of Calcutta's many years of feeling spiritually distant from God are another good example. Could one imagine a better modern-day example of a fervent disciple?

If we look to the Bible, we have only to imagine the life of one of God's most fervent followers, John the Baptist. John lived in the *desert*! The desert is the place of spiritual struggle, isolation, and difficulty. The place where one is stripped of all the conducive conditions for feeling fervent. John lived in the desert and was still filled with the Holy Spirit and extraordinary fervency. John preached *from the desert*! Even more telling, Jesus himself was "driven into the desert" by the Holy Spirit. The place of dryness, struggle, and temptation was the place where Jesus discovered who he was and what kind of messiah he would be. This reveals something we would not expect—that the Holy Spirit can live in the deserts of our lives.

Fervency is not only for those who have acquired a particular level of theological education. In our history of saints, we discover people like the towering intellectuals Aquinas and Augustine, but we also find St. Francis and Thérèse of Lisieux, who were not known for education or scholarship. All of these were fervent saints. We also cannot assume that fervent disciples have a particular theological or spiritual leaning or perspective that creates fervency. St. Teresa of Calcutta and Dorothy Day both saw Jesus

in the poor but also held very different social and political understandings of how to best address poverty and injustice.

It is also very important to know that fervent disciples are not
people who never have doubts or questions regarding their faith.
At the high point of Jesus' revelation of himself through his resurrection, we have his final appearance and revelation to his disciples at his ascension. At this extraordinary and intimate event of
the disciples with Jesus we read the following: "When they all saw
him, they worshiped, but they doubted" (Matthew 28:17). Even at
this sublime moment of divine revelation, right before their eyes,
the disciples still *doubted*. Too often many of us get caught up
in the trap of our doubts, recognition of life's complexities, and
living with so many theological nuances and ambiguities that we
begin to think we cannot carry these and still have fervency in our
discipleship. This is a dangerous trap that keeps many disciples
from fervency.

Lastly, fervent disciples are not those who never fail in their
discipleship. Again, we fall into the trap of thinking that because
we have failed at times, sometimes miserably, as a follower of Jesus
that we could never be fervent in the faith. Essentially, we are
saying to ourselves that "I am a loser" when it comes to discipleship. We only need to look to the Bible itself to free ourselves of
this kind of thinking. On the very eve of the resurrection was a
gathering of failed disciples! To this group of failures Jesus says:
"Peace be with you. As the Father sent me so I send you." Jesus
does not even address their utter failure in following him and
goes right into sending them forth as fervent disciples! Jesus is
assuming fervency is still possible, and in fact will happen, in
each of these disciples. Jesus acts in the same way toward us in
our many failures, because at the bottom line it is just not about

us; it is about the mercy and grace of God in Jesus, what Pope Francis calls, "a revolution of grace." When we get this, and move our focus off ourselves and onto the mercy and grace of God, we avoid these traps that keep us from fervency.

Where does fervency come from?

Michelangelo was once asked how he created his sculptures. He answered, "It's simple. I take a stone slab and knock off the extra pieces." Fervent disciples are created by knocking off the extra pieces. It is the disposition of the person of faith who sees, loves, and lives for what is essential. Jesus illustrated this when he spoke to Mary and Martha. "Martha, Martha, you are anxious and worried about many things. There is need of *only one thing*. Mary has chosen the better part and it will not be taken from her" (Luke 10:41–42). The problem with Martha was not that she was serving but that she had lost her focus; she was about "many things." Mary had already realized the "one thing," and it would not be taken from her. The "one thing" is Jesus!

PERSONAL REFLECTION

*What is the greatest obstacle in your life
to greater fervency in your faith?*

....

*What decision would you consider making
in your life right now that would help you
become a more intentional disciple?*

CHAPTER FOUR

LOVING JESUS

The one thing necessary…

Jesus himself brought us to the one thing when he spoke of the "one commandment": to love God with all our heart, with all our being, with all our strength, and with all our mind (Luke 10:27). Fervent disciples come from being in love with God through the person of Jesus. When I have encountered divine love for me personally, fervency begins to grow within my life. This encounter with divine love, which Paul says, "has been *poured* into our hearts through the Holy Spirit," is transformational. Now a person is "in motion," has a new direction, and is caught up in someone other and bigger than him- or herself. They discover a Christian faith that is not just about being nice, but about becoming "new"—a faith that is not just about doing religious activities as a maintenance of one's faith, but about being on fire with a mission, because you are on fire with a person.

Jesus again made this clear when, in the final words of John's gospel, after everything was said and done and the resurrected

Son of God was about to leave his disciples, Jesus turns to Peter and asks him, "Simon, son of John, do you love me?" Jesus asks this question three times. When one says one's final words in this life, they are usually words that reflect the essential and most important things they want to pass on to someone else. In this final scene in John's gospel, we do not find Jesus asking Peter if he will remain faithful to Jesus and keep the commandments, if Peter will do what he is commanded to do, or if Peter will live the disciplined life of faith. Instead Jesus asks Peter, "Do you love me?" To love Jesus is the one thing! It is this love of the person of Jesus that creates the fire of fervency and the power to live the vibrant life of faith.

Love involves an intimate encounter with another person

Jesus and the disciples lived together for about three years. Living with another person has the potential to develop intimacy. Jesus shared much of himself with the disciples during this time. In short, he was attempting to develop a loving, intimate relationship with his disciples. However, it was only after the resurrection that this intimacy with Jesus realized its fullest potential in their lives (as it does for us as well). We see this illustrated in the following passage:

> On the evening of that first day of the week, when the doors were locked, where the disciples were, for fear of the Jews, Jesus came and stood in their midst and said to them, "Peace be with you." And when he had said this, he breathed on them and said to them, "Receive the Holy Spirit."
> **JOHN 20:19, 22**
> *(In Greek and Hebrew, "spirit" means "breath.")*

Jesus breathed on his disciples. How intimate is breath? To breathe in the Spirit of Jesus is for the Spirit to become one with us, just as the air that fills our lungs becomes one with us. The intimacy and union with God that is given us is the source of our fire, our fervency, and our love for the one who so loves us. Breath permeates our entire being, and those dark places where we do not believe we could be loved or where God would never join us are precisely where Jesus most longs to join us. When we meet the risen Jesus in these dark places, we are never the same. When we have this encounter of divine love, we too, just as these first disciples, experience transformation into fervency.

The church fathers speak of the iron that is placed in the fire long enough that it takes on the color and heat of the fire. The iron has no heat of its own but it becomes the fire itself by being bathed in the fire. Everything in the Christian life is designed to set us on fire. The life of the church, all the prayer, sacraments, disciplines, are all designed for one purpose: to set us on fire with divine love, because divine love is itself a fire. The saints know this as well.

The poetry of St. John of the Cross beautifully expresses this:

Flame, alive, compelling,
Yet tender past all telling,
Reaching the secret center of my soul!

Ah! Gentle and so loving
You wake within me, proving
That you are there in secret and alone;
Your fragrant breathing stills me,
Your grace, your glory fills me
So tenderly your love becomes my own.

Too good to be true

One reaction to these words may be to think that this is a love reserved for saints or clergy or some other spiritual elite. Why do we think this? Every image of God in the Bible is of the fullness of God's generosity. Paul says the love of God is "poured" into our hearts. Nowhere do we read that God's generous love is parceled out, rationed, calculated, or stingy. In the parable of the sower of the seed, the seed is thrown everywhere in an extravagant, even wasteful manner. The multiplication of the loaves leaves behind twelve wicker baskets full of extra food after "they all ate and were satisfied" (Matthew 14:20). In Paul's letter to Titus we read, "For the grace of God has appeared, saving all" (Titus 2:11). The word is *all*, not some or the specially chosen.

The first miracle in John's gospel is the wedding feast where Jesus changes water into wine. What a beautiful symbol of the life, joy, and fullness that God brings to us in Jesus. A primary symbol of heaven throughout the Bible is the wedding feast. Weddings are always a place of abundance and excess and much more than one needs. We may struggle with this view of God's abundant love because it does not coincide with the societal demand that we keep our expectations and desires within realistic limits. As a result, we have trouble comprehending such an endless bounty. But where God is concerned, the problem lies in our desiring too little; growing in faith means expanding our expectations and we do this by *making God's generosity, God's boundless love, not our small stingy dispositions, the measure of our expectations.* These words can be transformational in how we think about God, by making God's generosity, not ourselves, the measure of our expectations.

Lovers know this

Those who are in love in a committed, healthy, life-giving way know this, and they know the love of the other is pure gift. The lover knows in a deep, visceral way that at some fundamental level, the love they have received is not about them ever deserving or earning the love. Love is in itself a mystery. Why does my lover love me so? When we take the focus off our personal weakness and poverty and place our focus on the generosity of God we can enter much more fully into this mystery of God's love.

That is why Paul and the saints speak of themselves as "the least," but this does nothing to hinder them from falling more in love with God because they know that their "worthiness" or "gift-edness" has never been the issue when it comes to God's love for them. God loves because God is Love. Those who love know the pure gift of the one who loves them and from this they discover joy. The "joy of the gospel" that Pope Francis speaks of.

Coming to know the supreme gift of God's love for us is beautifully expressed by Catherine of Siena:

> O fire of love! Was it not enough to gift us with creation in
> your image and likeness, and to create us anew to grace in
> your Son's blood, without giving us yourself as food, the
> whole of divine being, the whole of God? What drove you?
> Nothing but your charity, mad with love you are!
>
> F.N. SUZANNE NOFFKE, *THE PRAYERS OF CATHERINE OF SIENA*,
> PRAYER 10, P. 84 (SAN JOSE: AUTHORS CHOICE PRESS, 2001)

The great romance

The faith we are speaking of here is a love relationship with Jesus Christ. This is no small love. One could put it this way: "To fall in love with God is the greatest romance; to seek him the greatest adventure; to find him, the greatest achievement." The Bible puts it this way: "I will espouse you to me forever" (Hosea 2:21). Fervent disciples do not have a one-way relationship with God. They don't just encounter God's love and accept it. Fervent disciples are sustained by the reality that they are "in love with God"—they have a symbiotic relationship with God in which they give and receive love. And as they give more of themselves, more of their love, to God, they find that they receive far more than they could ever give. The best relationships between two people are much like this. In life people somehow find time in their schedule to be with the one they love. They change bad habits that annoy the loved one; they find themselves thinking of the loved one throughout the day, experience a new joy and energy in their lives, and in many cases become a better person, a better, healthier version of themselves. Why do we not see that this is the same reality we can experience in our relationship with God? Being "in love" with God would have the same effect, even more profound and long lasting.

In love with God

One of the best descriptions of faith, as being in love with God and the practical effects of this love, comes from Pedro Arrupe, SJ, former Superior General of the Jesuits.

> Nothing is more practical than finding God, that is, than
> "Falling in Love" in a quite absolute, final way. What you
> are in love with, what seizes your imagination, will affect
> everything. It will decide what will get you out of bed in the
> morning, what you do with your evenings, how you spend
> your weekends, what you read, who you know, what breaks

your heart, and what amazes you with joy and gratitude. Fall
in love, stay in love, and it will decide everything.

The life of a fervent disciple is characterized, "in a quite absolute,
final way," by being in love with God. This changes everything.
All of life is now animated, directed, stirred, and empowered by
the love of God. It is why we go to church, why we serve others,
why we seek forgiveness for our wrongs and attempt to repair the
wrongs of others. It is why we love and care for others even when
it is unpleasant and costly for us to do so. It is why people of
faith have joy when there is much conflict and pain in their lives
and why they have hope even in the face of darkness and death.
Falling in love with God is indeed everything! St. Catherine of
Siena put it this way, "You become what you love." This is what we
mean when we say that God's love is transformative.

Those who have been in love with another person know
something of the transformative nature of love itself. One example is my daughter, Hope. She is an absolutely wonderful person
whom I love with all my heart. Even though Hope has always had
many wonderful qualities, I noticed during her upbringing that
she never washed a dish without being asked. In fact, during her
adolescence, if you asked her to wash the dishes, she would give
you a look as if you had just asked her to donate a kidney. Today
Hope is an adult and married. When my wife and I visited her
and her husband in their first apartment, I noticed how Hope
acted when she was in the kitchen, by the sink, washing dishes.
She would smile and even hum a tune to herself. At first I thought
I was hallucinating. *What is this?* I thought to myself. *Where did this
come from?* Then I realized: she was in love. She was in love with
someone other than herself, and love changes everything. This is a

small example of the radical change that overcame the disciples in the upper room and that overcomes every disciple who encounters divine love personally in their lives—a love that St. Paul says empowers us to bear all things, believe all things, hope all things, and endure all things (1 Corinthians 13:7). A fervent disciple sees, loves, and lives for what is most essential: Jesus.

Don't people know this?

At this point, one might think, "Don't most people already know this?" Actually, many do not know this. How many of us were brought up with the understanding of faith as being in love with God? I was not. Additionally, many who do know this often keep it at a fairly superficial level, saying to themselves: "Let's not get carried away here." The result is that their life is not structured in such a way that their love relationship with Jesus Christ is attended to and given primary importance—the primary focus that love requires in order to flourish.

A brief review of our modern religious landscape illustrates how much this personal love relationship with Jesus is lacking.

Pew researchers revealed something startling about how many understand faith in terms of a "relationship" with God. The research revealed that nearly a third of Catholics believe in an impersonal God. Only sixty percent of Catholics believe in a personal God. Twenty-nine percent said that God is an "impersonal force." It would be pretty difficult to imagine a love relationship with an "impersonal force." Only forty-eight percent of Catholics were absolutely certain that the God they believed in was a God with whom they could have a personal relationship (Sherry Weddell, *Forming Intentional Disciples*).

I think we could press this question a little further if we were to ask those who profess a personal relationship with God how they would describe that relationship. To what extent is their personal relationship with God central to their lives? Is their personal relationship with God attended to in a regular, daily way, as any primary relationship would be? Is this relationship with God growing in intimacy? Would they consider themselves closer to God and more "in love with God" than they were a year ago? I believe these questions would be quite revealing as to the quality of the personal relationship with God that many believers have.

Are sacraments enough?

It would be safe to say that the majority of Catholics in the United States have received the sacraments of the church but have not received the person of the risen Jesus into their lives in a personally engaged way. Most practicing Catholics receive the sacraments and thereby are considered full adult members of the Catholic Church. At the same time that does not mean these Catholics have met Jesus and experienced his love for them. In other words, they have not been evangelized into the *kerygma* (*kerygma* means the very heart of the gospel, the core message of the Christian faith that all believers are called to proclaim). Sacraments are in and of themselves gifts of grace. When sacraments are received, grace is given to the person receiving the sacraments. Something of God is now present in the life of the recipient—as the pope puts it: the grace that gives "the capacity to believe." However, the capacity to believe is one thing, and choice is another. A gift can be given, but a gift may not be received. An example would be receiving a Christmas gift on Christmas morning. In the excitement and activity of the day the gift that you were given is placed by mistake in the closet. The gift you were given is still your gift, but this gift was never opened and never became part of your life. It is the same with sacraments; God's love is always freely given, but at the same time always requires our free response. As Augustine put it, "God will not save us without us."

What does it mean when someone says, "I am a Catholic"? Most likely they consider themselves members of the Catholic Church, "on the right team." They have received the sacraments, believe in God, and try to live a moral life. All good and all true. However, do they also see themselves as disciples of Jesus Christ in the midst of the church? Are their lives directed and animated by a personal love of Jesus, and are they involved in an ongoing process of formation and spiritual growth? That's how fervent disciples see themselves.

I think this equally applies to Christians from other faith traditions as well. Over the years I have been associated with a variety of Protestant and Evangelical Christians, many of whom profess and live a life of faith that is deep and vibrant, and who have often inspired and supported my own life of faith. At the same time, I have sometimes noticed that many Protestant and Evangelical Christians who refer to Jesus Christ as "my personal Lord and Savior" tend to focus on a past experience or moment that crystallized their faith: "I made a commitment of faith"; "I have given my life to Christ"; or "I have been born again." What happens in their life of faith after this event sometimes does not seem to be taken too seriously. Healthy relationships are dynamic not static, and they require a great deal of work to keep them that way. Relationships are either growing or declining based on the attention given and the intimacy shared.

A good analogy for what we are describing here is marriage. Why are some marriages vibrant and alive while other marriages are dull, with the couples having fallen into complacency in their relationship? The answer is that successful marriages have the ingredients in place that produce a successful relationship, and other marriages do not. I would suggest that good communication is the most critical and central part of a vibrant marriage and is in many ways the most important dimension of a healthy marriage. To have someone with whom you can share the most intimate parts of yourself, your deepest thoughts, feelings, yearnings, joys, and sorrows is a profound gift. (This also can happen in the context of deep, intimate friendship.) It is in the experience of this depth of communication that love grows, and this growth in love happens because you are continually being invited into a deeper intimacy with the other person. In short, you come to know the other more deeply. We can only love what we know, and we can only know what is communicated to us.

This is the same in the life of faith. Faith is a relationship with God, a relationship of love, and like all healthy, vibrant relationships, our relationship with God requires good communication. In the life of faith; that communication with God is called prayer.

PERSONAL REFLECTION

What do you think and how do you feel,
when you reflect on faith as "The Great Romance,"
as "falling in love with God"?

How could you be more open to
"falling in love" with God?

CHAPTER FIVE

A PERSONAL
ENCOUNTER
WITH JESUS

Faith is an encounter with Jesus. POPE FRANCIS

The fact that a personal, intimate encounter with the Divine is even possible is such extraordinary good news we may want to spend some time thinking about what this possibility offers us.

The words "personal encounter with Jesus" are foreign to many of us, particularly Catholics, and cause us to stop and think about how we understand our Christian faith. Many Catholics, myself included, were brought up to understand faith as "assent," an agreement with, or acceptance of, divine, revealed truth as articulated in church teaching. Most of us were not brought up with the language of a "personal encounter with Jesus," even if we in fact did possess the faith that this language reflects. Just how foreign this language is to many of us was driven home for me a few years ago.

I was speaking with one of our parishioners after Mass who said, "What I have noticed about our parish that is different from all the other parishes I have attended is that, at St. Norbert's, you speak a lot about Jesus." As one of the deacons, I smiled and received his words as a very encouraging compliment, but I couldn't help but feel a sense of sadness. It's unfortunate that talking about Jesus in our homilies is different, even novel, from all the other churches he'd attended. I understood what he meant, since this has been my experience as well. However, when you think about it, if you are preaching the gospel, what else is there to talk about? How sad it is when the proclamation of Jesus is a unique and novel experience. You cannot be fervent about that which you do not talk about.

This is Catholic

Another reason the language of encountering Jesus is difficult to comprehend is that many Catholics are honestly not sure whether or not they have encountered Christ in their lives. And if they haven't, they have no idea how such an encounter could happen for them. This is unfortunate, since everything in the Catholic spiritual tradition is essentially about a personal encounter with Christ. This "Catholic" encounter with Christ is not only the center of our deep, spiritual tradition of prayer but also is at the heart of each of the sacraments.

This is most clear in the Eucharist, where we receive (encounter) the very Body and Blood of the Person of Jesus Christ. Whether those receiving Christ in the Eucharist are open to an encounter with Christ in the Eucharist is another matter. But we believe that Christ is truly present and desires us to personally encounter him in the Eucharist, as well as in the proclamation of

God's word, in the presiding priest, and in the community of faith that is gathered around the Eucharist. This encounter with Christ is meant to happen every time we are at the celebration of Mass.

The entire sacramental life of the church is about a personal encounter with Christ. Each of the seven sacraments is an expression of belief in the Catholic faith community that essentially says, "God is here!" In each of these sacraments we are having an encounter with Christ within the community of faith called church.

The popes speak of encounter

St. John Paul II said that the aim of catechesis, the teaching of the faith, is that "the Christian, having accepted by faith the person of Jesus Christ as the one Lord and having given Him complete adherence by sincere conversion of heart, endeavors to know better this Jesus to whom he has entrusted himself" (*Catechesi Tradendae*, 20). "Only from a personal relationship with Jesus can an effective evangelization develop" (December 23/30, 1992. *L'Osservatore Romano* pp. 5–6).

Pope Benedict explained faith in this way: "Faith is above all a personal, intimate encounter with Jesus, and to experience his closeness, his friendship, his love; only in this way does one learn to know him ever more, and to love and follow him ever more." And while speaking to bishops in the Philippines in 2011, he noted that "your great task in Evangelization is therefore to propose a personal relationship with Christ as key to complete fulfillment."

In Pope Francis' first apostolic exhortation, *The Joy of the Gospel*, he writes: "I invite all Christians, everywhere, at this very moment, to a renewed personal encounter with Jesus Christ, or at least an openness to letting him encounter them; I ask all of you to do this unfailingly each day" (p. 1).

Analogy: Encountering Lincoln

What does it mean when we speak of a "personal encounter with Jesus"? A good way to understand the encounter with Jesus is to look at how we encounter people in our lives. There are several dimensions to encountering a person. For example, I love history, and one of my favorite historical figures is Abraham Lincoln. I am fascinated with and drawn to Lincoln as a person, and I read all that I can that he has written, what he said, and what others have said about all the dimensions of his life. I can say that through my study of Lincoln I have "encountered" him. I feel like I "know" him. At the same time, I have often wished that I could meet him, talk with him, and spend time with him. How I would love to hear him speak, hear his tone of voice and the inflection in his speech, and see the expressions on his face. I would love to hear him tell the stories and jokes that he is famous for sharing. This would be a much more significant "encounter" with Lincoln, and I would certainly come to know him better.

To take my encounter of Lincoln a step further, I have also wished that he and I could have developed a friendship. This friendship would occur if he and I spent time together, sometimes not even speaking much but just being together in one another's presence. For this friendship to go further, we would have times when we shared the contents of our hearts—one with another, Lincoln with me and I with him. I could imagine Lincoln talking with me about his depression, the difficulties in his marriage, and the profound grief he felt over the death of his sons. At the same time, I would speak with Lincoln of the joys, difficulties, and personal struggles within my own life. I could imagine his warm eyes looking at me as I spoke, and I believe he would create an environment of nonjudgmental acceptance toward me, that he would be a person that I could trust. The list of things that Lincoln and I could share with one another in the development of an intimate friendship can go on and on, with each new dimension deepening our friendship and furthering my personal encounter with Lincoln.

This encounter with Lincoln is a good analogy of how we can encounter Jesus in our lives today. Jesus can be encountered through the reading of the Bible and other commentaries about his life and person. However, an encounter with Jesus would be much more profound if we met him, walked with him, spent time with him, and communicated with him. "Jesus is risen" means that this is possible, that the living, real person of Jesus is alive and in our midst at all times. Jesus can be encountered in a deeply personal and self-revealing fashion. In John's gospel, Jesus calls us his friends, making clear the kind of personal encounter and relationship he is seeking with us. The Christian tradition of prayer and mystical encounter with the risen Christ speaks eloquently of such an encounter with Jesus. Our faith in Jesus is meant to be an intimate relationship that affects every aspect of our lives. We are meant to be intimate friends of Jesus and encounter him in all the dimensions that intimate friends encounter one another. This encounter of Jesus can happen in so very many ways in our human experience, and every human encounter with Jesus is uniquely personal and cannot be duplicated.

The analogy of my friendship with Lincoln eventually falls short, since the depths of our encounter with Jesus would be so much more than my encounter with Lincoln. The experience of intimate friendship is one thing, but our experience of Jesus is meant to be more like the union of marriage. With Jesus, the extent of sharing my joy and sorrows, the asking and receiving, the expressing of inner longing that could be shared encompasses the very depth of who I am. The intimacy of our encounter with Jesus is beyond what we could ask for or imagine.

Encountering Jesus in different ways
There is an extraordinary diversity of how this encounter with Jesus can occur in our lives. We spoke earlier of how often this encounter occurs in the midst of human suffering when the human heart is moved to cry out to God. As the psalmist says, "Out of the depths, I have cried to you, O Lord" (Psalm 130). However, there is also the subtle, almost imperceptible movement of grace in our lives. Someone recently said the following about their encounter with Jesus. "I do not know of any specific time or experience of God that gave me my faith. All I can say is that I have always believed in God; I have always loved God. I can even remember in eighth grade how during Lent I would skip lunch and walk to church, even when it was raining, just to spend time with God in prayer."

In our daily life there are also the simple, seemingly inconsequential ways that we encounter Jesus that we often miss or do not take seriously. Examples abound of the continual movement of God's loving reach toward us. Walking outside after a snowfall, standing on top of a mountain or before the ocean, watching the sun rise or set, listening to a song, reading a story, gazing upon great religious art, or watching a child at play can often be moments of encounter when our mind goes blank, time stops, and we are moved to silence or tears we do not understand. Every moment of our lives has the potential for a personal encounter with Jesus.

Finally, there are also those moments that come as surprise and with a drama that alters our lives. As one person related to me: "I was seventeen and having a typical day as a teenager, nothing out of the ordinary. I was in my room holding something in my hand when suddenly I powerfully experienced being held and enveloped in the love of God for me. I dropped what I was holding in my hand and stood there for several minutes. I knew I was in the grip of divine love. That was over thirty years ago, and I remember it as if it was yesterday."

How do we encounter Jesus?

Falling in love with God and experiencing a personal encounter with Jesus Christ happens first and foremost because God, in Jesus and through the Holy Spirit, loves us and pursues us in love. We know this because God "sent" his Son to be one of us: "I have come to seek and save the lost" (Luke 19:10). God in Jesus came to humanity to love us and save us from sin and death. The initiative is with God, not with us. It is the same in our personal lives. God knows each of us by name. He has numbered the hairs on our head, and God is pursuing us as a lover toward the beloved. This is a most important reflection and starting point for us who desire to grow in this intimate love of God in our personal lives. Seeing God in this way creates a disposition of openness and receptivity, not one of frantic search and anxiety over the outcome. Mary is the model disciple in the Bible, and her words are most illustrative here: "Let it be done to me." In other words, *Let it come. Let love love. Let me receive you into my heart, my mind, my soul, my body.* This disposition of "yielding" in prayer and in our life is most central and necessary for us to experience the love of God and to encounter Jesus personally in our life.

At the same time, we are created with human freedom, the freedom to accept or reject this love. This leaves us with a mystery of the interplay of grace and human freedom, and we can only wonder why some of us know God's intimate love, while others do not. We often assume that a person has faith and another doesn't because of the influences on their life and upbringing. We think that someone has faith because they had good parents and a family that lived their faith, inspirational teachers along the way, or a solid Catholic education. While all of these are potentially sources of faith, we also know many people who have had these benefits and do not have faith. I often feel a sense of awe and am deeply moved when I consider why I have faith, because in the final analysis I do not have a rational answer. I can only be in awe of the mystery of God's merciful love for me. It is like the seed that grows by itself into a plant. Even the best gardener in the world still cannot convert the seed into a plant. She or he can only create conducive conditions for this "miracle" to happen.

≈⑂⑂≈

PERSONAL REFLECTION

*Can you think of a time in your life where
you had a personal encounter with Jesus?*

....

*As you look back on your life, can you begin
to see ways that God has pursued you,
which you may have missed?*

CHAPTER SIX

HAVING A PLAN TO ENCOUNTER JESUS

While there are a multitude of ways to encounter Jesus, it is important to have a focus, a plan, or a program in our life that helps to facilitate this encounter. When a gardener plants a seed in the ground he knows he cannot make the seed germinate and grow, because it comes about as a gift, beyond our control. But he also knows that by creating the right conditions for germination, the potential for this growth, this life, is greatly increased. It is the watering, fertilizing, and sunlight offered to the plant that is essential to its growth. Thomas Merton put it this way: "All we can do with any spiritual discipline is produce within ourselves something of the silence, the humility, the detachment, the purity of heart, and the indifference which are required if the inner self is to make some shy, unpredictable manifestation of his presence"

(*The Inner Experience: Notes on Contemplation*, p. 7). Here are some thoughts on how to create conditions that greatly increase our potential for personally encountering Jesus.

Pope Francis' plan

On the first page of his apostolic exhortation *The Joy of the Gospel*, Pope Francis lays out a five-step program for opening ourselves to an encounter with Jesus.

POPE FRANCIS' FIVE STEP PLAN TO ENCOUNTER JESUS CHRIST

1. Openness
2. Daily Commitment
3. Way of Thinking
4. Risk
5. Repentance

These steps may seem simple, but they are powerful, urgent advice:

> I invite all Christians, everywhere, at this very moment, to a renewed personal encounter with Jesus Christ, or at least an openness to him encountering you; to do this unfailingly each day. No one should think that this invitation is not meant for him or her, since "no one is excluded from the joy brought by the Lord." The Lord does not disappoint those who take the risk; whenever we take a step towards Jesus, we come to realize he is already there, waiting with open arms. Now is the time to say to Jesus; "Lord, I have let myself be deceived; in a thousand ways I have shunned your love, yet here I am once more, to renew my covenant with you. I

need you. Save me once again, Lord, take me once more into
your redeeming embrace."

1. BE OPEN

"At least an openness to him encountering you."
While the gift of faith and encountering Jesus is primarily a movement of God toward us—it is God who takes the initiative and
seeks us out—it does require a disposition of "openness" on our
part to allow this encounter to happen. When Nicodemus comes
to Jesus in John's gospel, we find him coming at night. Darkness
is a biblical image of unbelief, yet at the same time Nicodemus
is coming toward the light, toward Jesus. This is a biblical expression of the kind of "openness" to Jesus that is the required disposition of those who are seeking to encounter him in a new way.
How beautiful are the pope's words in this regard: "or at least an
openness to him encountering you." This takes a lot of pressure
off of us in our desire to encounter Jesus. We do not make this
encounter happen, and it is not about any particular technique
or how well we do in our attempts to encounter Jesus. It is ultimately a gift of God's grace and love toward us. All we essentially
do is show up and be open to receiving Jesus anew in our lives. In
the pope's words, all we need to say is: "here I am once more." Be
open and you will encounter Jesus.

2. DAILY

"Do this unfailingly each day."
The life of faith and our encounter with the risen Jesus is not a
one-and-done experience. The reason the journey of faith is so
adventurous and at times thrilling is because it never ends and

only gets more wonderful and profoundly impactful in our lives. There is always more. We can all identify with Nicodemus: we all come with some "unfaith," some aspect of our person that is still in darkness, and we need to come toward the light over and over, every day. It is this regular commitment to prayer and seeking Jesus that changes everything.

3. HOW YOU THINK
"No one should think this invitation is not meant for him or her."
In the New Testament, the word used for "conversion" means to "have a new mind." Not only does our encounter with Jesus transform our hearts, it is meant to transform our minds, the way we think and perceive ourselves, others, God, and life itself. There is a significant tendency within many of us to write off our capacity to encounter Jesus because of how we think of ourselves. We say, "I am just an average person. I am not very spiritual." The way we think about ourselves in relation to God and our capacity for encountering God can severely limit our encounter with Jesus.

4. RISK
"The Lord does not disappoint those who take the risk."
Faith, like love, always involves risk. At the heart of faith and openness to encountering Jesus is trust. In the gospels the expression Jesus himself utters about faith is almost exclusively a call away from fear, and to trust. "Fear is useless; what is needed is trust" (Luke 8:50). These words should be written on our screen savers and placed on the refrigerator because they express the most important disposition of the human heart regarding our openness, or lack thereof, to encountering Jesus in our lives.

5. REPENTANCE

"Now is the time to say to Jesus; 'Lord, I have let myself be deceived; in a thousand ways I have shunned your love, yet here I am to renew my covenant with you. I need you. Save me once again, Lord, take me once more into your redeeming embrace."

Pope Francis beautifully expresses the central place for encountering Jesus in our lives: mercy. The encounter of human sinfulness and divine mercy is an encounter like no other in the human experience. It is the greatest source of personal transformation in our lives. How wonderful is the Christian belief that no human sinfulness is not already forgiven by God. How accessible is our encounter with the God of mercy when all we need to do is to acknowledge our denial of God's love and to come "once more into your redeeming embrace." As St. Teresa of Ávila put it so well: "All we need to do to begin again, is to begin again."

In reflecting on these five steps, it is important to see how they all go together. Developing a disposition within ourselves that is open, trusting, seeking, accepting, and willing to bring every obstacle to this encounter to him is the way of life for the fervent disciple who encounters the love of God in Jesus over and over along the journey of faith.

⇝⇜

PERSONAL REFLECTION

What aspect(s) of the above plan do you need in your life?

....

Is there something you would add to this five-step plan?

CHAPTER SEVEN

PRAYER

*We need heralds of the Gospel who are
experts in humanity, who know the depths
of the human heart, who can share the joys, the hopes,
the agonies, the distress of people today, but who are,
at the same time, contemplatives who have
fallen in love with God.* SAINT JOHN PAUL II

Why pray?

The answer is the same as the answer to why we do all things
"Christian": because we love God (or because we want to love
God). Faith is the experience of God's love, the personal encounter with the one who loves us. Like all successful love relationships, we discover that our love grows when our knowledge of the
other grows, and our knowledge of the other grows by how well
and often we communicate with the other—in this case, God.
And prayer is how we communicate with God. That is why prayer
is central, even critical, to the life of faith, especially when we
see faith as a personal relationship with Jesus, the Father, and the

Holy Spirit. More than anything else, the intimacy that we create with God through our prayerful communication will determine the vibrancy of our faith and the fervency of our discipleship. Prayer is the primary place where we experience the "renewed personal encounter with Jesus Christ" that Pope Francis is urging us toward.

Consider this story about a party in London many years ago. In attendance was a well-known Shakespearean actor and an old, faithful Christian missionary. During the event people asked the actor to recite something for them. He replied that he would recite Psalm 23, but only if the missionary also recited the Psalm for everyone. The missionary was shy and initially refused, but after some coaxing he agreed. The actor went first: "The lord is my shepherd; there is nothing I shall want..." Those gathered were captivated by the eloquence of the actor's oratory and all applauded and complimented him when he finished. Then it was the missionary's turn. Pausing in silence before he began, he recited slowing, prayerfully, and from his heart, allowing his words to reflect his lived experience over many years of Jesus as "his shepherd." "The Lord is my Shepherd, there is nothing I shall want..."

When the missionary finished there was silence throughout the room, tears filled the eyes of many of the listeners. The actor broke the silence and said, "That, ladies and gentlemen, is the difference between knowing something *about* the shepherd and *knowing* the shepherd."

That, friends, is the life of faith, the gift of intimacy with God in Jesus given to us, and prayer is the way we receive and grow in this intimacy every day. This is the first reason why we pray.

The second reason we pray, which is often missed and is more profound than we realize, is that Jesus prayed. Over and over we read in the Bible that Jesus went off alone to pray. The Scriptures suggest that personal prayer for Jesus was daily—in the early morning, a regular, committed, sustained, daily time of prayer. I think if Jesus understood prayer as a priority in his life, as something essential that he needed, then we just might need prayer as well.

I often wonder what it must have looked like to the disciples, who would see Jesus at prayer and watch him when he returned. In Luke 11:1 we read, "Jesus was praying in a certain place, and when he finished, one of his disciples said to him, 'Lord, teach us how to pray.'" What did it look like to see Jesus in prayer only a short distance away? What did his face look like when he returned to his disciples after he spent time in prayer with his Father? It must have been captivating for the onlooking disciples. So they ask, "Lord, teach us how to pray." Essentially, they are saying, "Give us what you have."

Jesus did give them what he had, the very relationship that Jesus had with his Father Jesus gave to his disciples, and Jesus gives this relationship to us as well. In fact, Jesus longs to give us the same relationship with his Father that he has. "As you, Father, are in me and me in you, that they also may be in us" (John 17:21). This is why prayer is the essential first ingredient, the foundation, for the life of a fervent disciple. Prayer is how we grow in the love of God in our lives.

Obstacles to prayer

There are many common obstacles to developing prayer in our life. We are all prone to experience most of these at some point in our life and thoughts about prayer.

1. Time

The most common reason given for not praying is, "I don't have the time!" A response from the Bible would be: "Where your treasure is, there your heart will be." I remember someone saying to me they don't mind being asked to give money to the church or a good cause, but when asked to give their time, well, they get very defensive and say no. But this same person finds time for golf, watching football, going to the movies, reading the paper, listening to the evening news, and lots of other things. He also goes to church on Sunday. Fervent disciples know that life is a gift and that our lives are not our own. Fervent disciples also know that our primary calling in life is to love God and our neighbor. Fervent disciples may play golf, go to the movies, and engage in many of the activities listed above, but they also know that everything is secondary to their relationship with Jesus. They prioritize their lives and their days so that they leave time for their important relationships. And what relationship is more important than the one we have with God?

There is another great truth about prayer and time. Whatever time we give to God in prayer it will be given back many times over. This was very well expressed by philosophy professor Peter Kreeft who wrote in his book *Prayer: The Great Conversation*:

> We have time and prayer backwards. We think that time determines prayer, but prayer determines time. We think our lack of time is the cause of our lack of prayer, but our lack of prayer is the cause of our lack of time. When the little boy offered Christ five loaves and two fishes, he multiplied them miraculously. He does the same with our time, but only if we offer it to him in prayer. This is literally

miraculous, yet I know from repeated experience that it happens. Every day that I say I am too busy to pray, I seem to have no time, accomplish little, and feel frazzled and enslaved to time. Every day that I say I'm too busy not to pray, every time I offer some time-loaves and life-fishes to Christ, he miraculously multiplies them, and I share in his conquest of time. I have no idea how he does it, but I know that he does it, time after time.

I too have seen this time and time again in my own life, and you will too. Discipleship is a choice, an everyday choice, and prayer is the source that makes discipleship not only possible but vibrant.

2. Unnecessary

People often resist the idea of a specific routine of daily prayer because they say it is unnecessary and that God is everywhere and with us always, so we can talk to God anytime we want. Well, yes! Please do! But without setting aside a designated time to pray, it becomes all too easy to forget or to become lazy or complacent. Chip Kelly, former head coach of the Philadelphia Eagles football team, is known for using short, inspirational quotes to help his team. The one he used his first year is, "Habits reflect the mission." He is saying that everything a player on the team does, in his personal life, how he relates to teammates off the field, and how he approaches the game of football should all be done to reflect and help achieve the mission. The same applies to fervent disciples. The disciple who loves God and wants to serve God will create routine habits that reflect the mission he or she has as a follower of Christ.

Let's use the example of marriage again. If spouses think they do not need regular time alone with their partner to communicate but assume they can just fire off an email during the day or rely on the occasional phone call to check in, eventually that relationship starts to erode and lose the sense of intimacy and closeness it once had. Marriage counselors know that couples with a regularly scheduled time to share and communicate tend to have a much healthier relationship than those who don't and instead think, "I'll get around to it later."

3. Nothing happens

Another objection to prayer is that "nothing happens" when we pray, so why bother? Here's a brief example from my own life. There was a time when I had fallen out of shape physically, and so I decided to start running every day. The first day I began by running around the block on which I live. I was about a quarter of the way around the block when I thought I was going to die. I thought to myself, "This is awful, painful, and I don't know if I can keep this up every day." The next day, I ran again and got about ten feet further than the first day before the near-death experience began to set in again. The third day, the process repeated itself: ten more feet, death, walk home. The following week, I made it around the entire block; I was very proud of myself, and the death experience began to lose its grip on me. (I also must add that this was a very, very long block. Probably the longest block in the world, I am sure.) Eventually what happened is that as I ran every day the pain went away and I ran further and further. I remember thinking how much better I felt throughout the day because of the exercise and how much I began to enjoy the running; I even began looking forward to it. Everything had changed.

It is the same with prayer. Not every prayer time will be easy or seemingly beneficial, but over time the benefits build up, like exercising or eating healthy. There may not be instant gratification, but every time we pray we are improving our spiritual life a little bit at a time.

No one says this better than Henri Nouwen when he writes in his book *Daybreak*:

> Why should I spend an hour in prayer when I do nothing
> during that time but think about people I am angry with,
> people who are angry with me, and thousands of other silly
> things that happen to grab my mind for a moment?
>
> The answer is: because God is greater than my mind
> and my heart, and what is really happening in the house
> of prayer is not measurable in terms of human success and
> failure. What I must do is be faithful.
>
> The remarkable thing, however, is that sitting in the
> presence of God for one hour each morning—day after day,
> week after week, month after month—in total confusion
> and with myriad distractions radically changes my life.

Essentially what Nouwen is saying is that we need to avoid the strong tendency within us to evaluate, categorize, and judge our prayer. In short, all prayer is good, worthwhile, and beneficial. This may be hard for us to accept. The movement of our mind seeks to evaluate, understand, and categorize, and this does not work with prayer.

The call to prayer is a call to God, to love God with all our heart, mind, soul, and strength. The one who loves comes to know the absolute primacy and necessity of being with the one we love, even if it seems at times that we are alone and no one is listening.

4. *I'm not that spiritual*

Many people think that prayer is reserved for a certain kind of person, a spiritual commando who can easily connect with God. People often think that they are just "not that spiritual." They say to themselves: "I'm a practical, everyday kind of person, down to earth, not programmed for this sort of thing." They begin to think that their personal prayers are just not that good. That the prayers that other people say or that they hear in church are just so much better. The result is not to trust the prayer from our heart, in our words, to God.

Imagine a young child in grade school who on Mother's Day or Father's Day is asked to draw a picture and write a card for their parent. Now imagine the child coming home and presenting the card to her mother or father, saying, "Mom/Dad, you know I am not good at writing words so I asked Sally to write the words, and you know I am not very good at drawing so I asked Tommy to draw the picture on the front. So, here is your Mother's Day/Father's Day card." No. No! No parent would want that. What they want is their child's words, their child's picture. They passionately want the simple, scribbled, messy words and picture from the child. Because the card is from their child, the card is "PERFECT." The child's words and picture are so very, very pleasing to the parent.

No good parent would say, "You know you drew outside the lines and your colors didn't match and you misspelled a word." No, what parents do with these cards is save them and cherish them. (I have a whole box of them from my children.) In fact, what a parent often does is put the card and the picture on the refrigerator, and when someone comes over to the house they proudly show off the card their child made for them. I am pretty sure that God has a great big refrigerator in heaven. You see, all our prayers, all of our prayers, are precious to God. All prayers from our heart are perfect for God. We are God's children, God is our father. We pray as humans, as God's children, not as angels. If God only wanted the prayer of angels, he would have only made angels. We are God's children, and God wants nothing more than "our" prayer. Every prayer is precious to God.

We can all pray

We must also get over the thinking that only certain people can really pray. Here is the good news about prayer—we can all do it; we can all pray! Thomas Merton says it well:

> Nothing anyone says (in prayer) will be important. The great thing is prayer. Prayer itself. If you want a life of prayer, the way to get to it is by praying. We have to start where we are. We were indoctrinated so much into means and ends that we don't realize that there is a different dimension in the life of prayer. In prayer we discover what we already have. You start where you are and you deepen what you already have, and you realize that you are already there. We already have everything, but we don't know it and we don't experience it. Everything has been given to us in Christ. All we need is to experience what we already possess. (Meeting at Our Lady of the Redwoods Abbey in California; article by David Steindl-Rast, "Recollections of Thomas Merton's Last Days in the West," in *Monastic studies 7*.)

Growing in prayer: "Take the time"

Thomas Merton was once asked, "How do I grow in prayer?"

Merton's response, "Take the time." Three words that express the most important aspect in growing in prayer: "take the time!"

The most important decision a person of faith can make to grow as a fervent, intentional disciple is the decision to pray every day. For many of us, this may require scheduling a daily appointment that is given the highest priority. Begin with twenty minutes at the same time and same place each day.

I have been recommending this for over forty years, and no one I know who has tried this with sincerity has said it didn't work for them. This is the first and most important decision for someone who wants to grow in a faith that is vibrant and in a discipleship that is fervent. People who pray grow. They grow in faith and closeness to God. They begin naturally praying more throughout the day, and they begin recognizing God's presence and experiencing the fruits of the Spirit: the love, peace, and joy of God.

There is nothing so special or so spiritual here. It is a simple decision to love God first before all things, in prayer. Therefore, we give God quality time, not when we are tired, distracted, and ready for bed but the time of day when we are most emotionally and psychologically ready to engage with life. For most people, this comes first thing in the morning. Jesus himself gave prayer the highest priority and the best time he had: "Rising early in the morning, He went off to a solitary place in the desert; there he was absorbed in prayer" (Mark 1:35–37).

Fasting from noise

Giving God quality time also means fasting from noise. In our modern world, this has become increasingly difficult. Just to be silent is very hard for us, but silence is the place for prayer, because silence slows down our racing minds. And avoiding noise includes not only the sounds of our world but the little gadgets and screens that beep and flash at us, demanding our attention. (Setting this time aside may be difficult for someone like the mother of very young children. Here is a tip: when you are in the car and the children are quiet, turn off the radio and let the car become your place of prayer as you turn your mind and heart toward God. When we desire to find the time for prayer we often do, even when there is much to distract us.)

A pastor in a church in England noticed a woman who would enter the church and sit in the last pew every day at the same time. At first it seemed she was reading something she held in her lap, but after some time she would come in the same time every day and just sit quietly in silence. After some time, the pastor came up to her and said how delighted he was to see her come in every day for prayer. The women responded, "Oh no, well at least not in the beginning. You see, the stop for the bus I take is just outside this church, and it is so cold outside that I initially came in just to stay warm while I waited. In the beginning, I would sit here and go through the things in my purse. After some time, however, I noticed something happening to me. Just sitting in silence, every day, began to have an effect on me. It drew me to something I had never done much of; I began to think about God, and yes, eventually I began to pray. Now that is what I do when I come in here each day."

It was the silence, the daily silence that had the effect on this woman. Sitting in silence is in and of itself a potentially trans-formative activity. Something that can be very difficult in the beginning will eventually be something we long for. That is the tradition of silent prayer that Jesus himself, John the Baptist, and the saints all understood.

This commitment to daily prayer is eloquently expressed in the words of Joseph Cardinal Bernardin in his book *The Gift of Peace*.

> I learned many years ago that the only way I could give quality time to prayer was by getting up early in the morning. (I must add parenthetically that I didn't have a great desire to get up so early.) In the early hours of the morning, before the phones and doorbells started to ring, before the mail arrived, seemed to me to be the best for spending quality time with the Lord. So I promised God and myself that I would give the first hour of each day to prayer. This doesn't mean that I have not experienced the struggles that other people have faced. Quite the contrary. But early on, I made another decision. I said, Lord, I know that I spend a certain amount of that morning hour of prayer daydreaming, problem-solving, and I'm not sure that I can cut that out. I'll try, but the important thing is, I'm not going to give that time to anybody else. So even though it may not connect me as much with you as it could, nobody else is going to get that time.

This kind of intentionality and commitment to prayer reflects and creates the fervent disciple.

What is prayer?
There are many definitions of prayer. I will suggest one from what I think is a good source, St. Teresa of Ávila, the great sixteenth-century mystic and one of the most influential and extraordinary writers on prayer. Teresa defines prayer as this: "Nothing more

than the friendly conversation in which the soul speaks heart-to-heart with one we know loves us."

"Friendly conversation" means that we all can do this! We all know what it is like to speak with another person. However, there is a certain quality to this conversation; it is "heart to heart." While we can speak to God about anything, I think God is more concerned with the matters of our heart than anything else. I once worked with someone who would greet me and then ask, "How is your heart?" At first I thought this a little weird, but after some time began to appreciate what he was asking. He really wanted to get to know me, really wanted a relationship of substance with me. In time I began to share with him how my heart was and we became good friends. I then began to ask my children at home the same question, "How is your heart?" I am sure, at first, they thought I was a little weird, but in time they too began to understand what I was asking and why, and they too began to respond. Do we really want relationships in which we only talk about the weather and sports? Is that a relationship of substance? Is that why we gather as church? Or is church and discipleship the sharing of our life with another, the light and the darkness, the joys and the sorrows? This is what God wants from us, our hearts. In prayer we are to speak from our hearts to God. We have nothing to fear since we speak to the one we know loves us.

I often think how foolish it is to go to God in prayer and in a pious fashion pretend God doesn't see things. We think somewhat unconsciously that if we don't bring it up then God doesn't see it. We all have some fear of intimacy, of sharing the contents of our heart with another, but this is the very goal and purpose of prayer. It is the source of our falling in love with God. We have one in whom we can trust; this is the essence of Christian faith, to trust God. Over three hundred times we read in the New Testament "do not be afraid" and over and over, "trust me." What do we have to fear, for "it is your Father who sees what is in secret" (Matthew 6:4)? Remember: It is "your Father." Your Father is the one who sees it all and loves us just the same.

Ultimately it is not really that important how we define prayer or how we pray. What is essential is that we pray, every day, and that our prayer entails the opening of our hearts to the love of our Father, the Father "who sees what is in secret" and loves us.

Prayer begins or has already begun in you, because you are reading this book. The desire to pray is a prayer itself and is a sign of God already within you. Follow this desire, this movement; go with it! When you want to pray, you will pray, by turning this desire toward God. It is that simple. Begin by turning your whole self, your mind, heart, body, sexuality, and emotions, all of you, toward God. It all begins with attentiveness to this inner desire and longing for God. It really all begins with God.

PERSONAL REFLECTION

What was your prayer like
when you were younger?

....

What is your prayer like now?

....

What would you like your
prayer to become?

CHAPTER EIGHT

PRAYER: A PRACTICAL GUIDE

Practical guide to P.R.A.Y.

PRAISE *"Our father, who art in heaven, holy is your name."*

REPENTANCE *"Forgive us our sins as we forgive those who have sinned against us."*

ASK *"Give us this day our daily bread."*

YIELD *"Thy kingdom come, thy will be done on earth as it is in heaven."*

P.R.A.Y. is offered as a simple guide through a time of personal prayer. This is not a "how to pray" but a way of giving focus to your prayer. It is given as a response to the question, "What do I do when I pray?" You will find these four aspects of prayer throughout the Scriptures and in the very prayer that Jesus gave us to pray, the Our Father. It is easy to remember and many people, myself included, have found this to be a very helpful tool for daily prayer.

P...PRAISE

"Our Father, who art in heaven, holy is your name."
A good way to begin a time of prayer is to give God praise. We can begin by simply thanking and praising God for his love, goodness, and grace in our lives. We do this because it is true that God is good—love itself—and freely gives us his love, and we do this so we can get our focus correct. It is God we are speaking to, and this changes the nature of the conversation from how we would speak to another human being. God deserves our praise and thanks, but God does not need it; we do. When we praise God we get caught up a little more in God and leave ourselves and our self-preoccupation. I often begin prayer with praise and thanks and then I speak to God from my heart. I may sing a hymn out loud softly or within my mind quietly. I may read a psalm of praise. Here we acknowledge our struggles and at the same time acknowledge the goodness, faithfulness, and power of God. This is a good time to cultivate "wonder," to meditate on the greatness of God, the vastness of the universe, the billions of humans on the earth, and the wonder of nature.

R...REPENTANCE

"Forgive us our sins as we forgive those who have sinned against us."
We all have damaged relationships and endure conflict with other people, with ourselves, and with God. In healthy relationships we

go to the one we have hurt, or they come to us when we have hurt them. We deal with the truth of our mistakes, faults, and lack of love. When we do this, we grow and our relationships grow, and we find peace and reconciliation. Healthy relationships do this in a regular way, and so do fervent disciples. If we are in love with God we want nothing to damage or interfere with that relationship, so we regularly repent and seek forgiveness from the one we know loves us.

In prayer, we resolve our "personal conflicts" with God, with ourselves, and with our neighbor. We examine our conscience to see what may be an obstacle in any of the three areas (God, self, others) that we need to prayerfully consider and perhaps become reconciled with or make an action plan to address. Without this examination and openness to repentance, our prayer can fall into something dangerous and dysfunctional. Prayer becomes a time to seek some personal comfort; we manipulate our prayer into a sense of being "religious" and "good" and keeping us from dealing with the realities of our lives. Prayer is meant to be the very opposite of denial. It is the place where we spend time in "truth"—the truth of God's love and mercy for us that frees us from the fear of accepting our own limitations and the reality of all human brokenness. One might ask during this time of prayer:

- Lord, what is keeping me from trusting you?
- Where is fear still directing my life?
- How can I love you, how can I love others, as you love me?
- Where am I blind to my own self-centeredness?
- What is this anger and resentment telling me and what do I do with it?
- How do I pray and act in a world filled with so much suffering, sin, and injustice?

We cannot grow in prayer and intimacy with God if we are holding resentment or remain blind to our own actions and dispositions of un-love toward others.

A…ASK

"Give us this day our daily bread."

"Oh, I already ask God for too much." That is the common response when I suggest we seek God through intercession in prayer. It is good to remember that "asking," petitioning, God is the most common form of prayer in the New Testament. The gospel story of the "unjust judge" makes it clear that God not only has no problem with our asking, but actually encourages us to seek his help, even to an excessive degree. Intercessory prayer is not our attempt to control or manipulate God. Intercession is our seeking God's help in love for ourselves and others, and for social justice. We are asking that God's will be done, that God's purposes and kingdom may be present a little more on earth.

Remember, everything we do in Christianity is about love. Love is neither controlling nor manipulative; love seeks the good of the other. When we understand that asking God for help is a high form of loving, it changes our understanding of the nature of intercessory prayer. Intercessory prayer is self-less and offered for the sake of the community, to God, through Christ in the Spirit. It is prayer for the kingdom of God to come and overcome the violence and injustice in our world. In a very real sense our intercessory prayer is participating in the redemptive work of Christ and is therefore a central way that we serve, minister, and bring forth the kingdom of God.

"If you had the faith of a mustard seed you could say to this mountain be lifted up and cast into the sea and it would be done for you" (Matthew 17:20). God is not really concerned with casting mountains into the sea. This helps no one. But God is very concerned with overcoming sin, evil, injustice, power, and violence. These are the mountains that God is looking for people of prayer to move! Fervent disciples have a sense of this power given to them in prayer, and they pray in intercession as much as possible out of love of God and neighbor.

Y...YIELD

"Thy kingdom come, thy will be done on earth as it is in heaven."
Now we come to the last, most difficult, and crucially important element of prayer—yielding to God. This is where we surrender to God and give over everything into God's loving care. Yielding to God is to let everything go and just *be* with God. Here we open our hearts and minds as places of receptivity, to listen and to receive what will come to us from the one who loves us. This is the place of "listening silence" where we free our minds of all thinking and just be, just feel, just receive, allowing ourselves to be fully vulnerable and open even if just for a few minutes or seconds. Here we "dial down" into silence. I might say this is where we "stop" praying and let God pray within us. We try to completely quiet the mind. If your mind must go somewhere, let it focus on the words of a hymn that you very slowly sing in your mind, or a slowly repeated prayer—"In you I place my trust, O Lord...In you I place my trust," or one line from Scripture that helps you to pray; or even better, just focus on your breathing, and after some time, focus on the Spirit praying within you.

The idea here is to become "mind-less" so we can become "mind-full." Now we wait and see what happens, what sensations or experience of God's presence we feel, perhaps what thoughts come to us. This type of prayer is very difficult for us and must be cultivated, but it is the goal of all prayer to "be with the one who loves us," and to commune in the silence of that love where God is in charge and we are fully open to his love. It is similar to when two people in love gaze into each other's eyes or a parent looks into the eyes of their young child. Prayer is this intimate communion. There are no thoughts racing through their minds. They are simply gazing into the eyes of the one they love. This is as good as it gets in prayer this side of heaven.

As you consider these aspects of prayer, remember not to be rigid; be open to the flow of your prayer. Each one of the above dimensions of prayer will vary in time and intensity each time you pray. One day your prayer may be filled with praise and little else. Another day it is asking. Some days may be a little of each. Just go with the flow. Your life experience changes every day, and so does the focus of your prayer. Every time you pray, even if for just a minute or two, spend time yielding to God. This area needs the most practice and is the goal of all we do in prayer.

PERSONAL REFLECTION

What aspect of the above guide to prayer
do you find the most helpful?

....

What aspect is the most challenging? Why?

CHAPTER NINE

HOW DO WE HEAR GOD?

God speaks in the silence of the heart,
and we listen. And then we speak to God
from the fullness of our heart, and God listens.
And this listening and this speaking
is what prayer is meant to be.

SAINT TERESA OF CALCUTTA

Hearing aids

Fervent disciples are people of faith who are led by the Holy Spirit. In the Bible, especially in the Acts of the Apostles, this is so common that we get the impression that it is normal and taken for granted as the way disciples operate—a kind of *modus operandi*. Almost anywhere you turn in the Acts of the Apostles you find this. Chapter 13, verse 4 begins with, "So they, sent forth by the Holy Spirit…" Only nine lines later we read, "Paul, filled with the Holy Spirit, looked intently at him and said…" Where the apostles went and what they said were all guided by the Holy Spirit. People just don't talk like that anymore. It seems to be a missing element in contemporary Christian experience, and it begs the question: why?

One answer is clear: this is not easy. How does one know that it is the Holy Spirit leading them and not their own agenda, ego, wants, or wishes misinterpreted as the Holy Spirit? This is a good question. But because it is difficult to answer does not mean we cannot come to understand how this operates in the life of a fervent disciple.

This question is even more important when we consider the nature of prayer itself. Even the definition we are using here, from Teresa of Ávila—"Nothing more than the friendly conversation in which the soul speaks heart-to-heart with one we know loves us"—begs the question: If prayer is a "friendly conversation" with God, then how do we hear God's part in the conversation? If faith is defined as a relationship, and all relationships must be "two-way," where is God's voice? If vibrant faith comes from being in love with God, and love must come from knowing the other, and knowing comes from communication with the other, then how does God communicate himself to us? If communication is talking and listening, then this is the "listening" part. The listening in prayer is never easy, and good communication is a lot of work, but it can happen.

God does speak to us

Let us begin with the extraordinary claim that "God speaks to us." Many take this for granted, but it is really an exceptional gift and grace that this even happens at all. We are saying that the God of the cosmos cares so much for each one of us personally that this cosmic

God has numbered the hairs on our heads and desires to guide us in our daily lives. This alone is enough for great awe and joy.

Why does God speak to us? There is only one reason: love. *God loves us.* Of course, a God like this would answer his children who cry out to him, speak to his children who listen to him, and come to his children who long for him and wait for him with anxious and loving hearts. We know this must be true, since the very center of Christian faith is that God sent his Son into the world to love the world and to "communicate" this love to all humanity. Yes, hearing God speak can be tricky to figure out. Many might say: *Jesus did come on this earth to reveal God to us, but he is raised now and God is pure spirit. Jesus is no longer in the flesh, so how can we ever really hear God speak unless God uses human words?*

Consider the following example. When I was in college I decided to go to live and study in Germany for one year. I did so to learn the German language. I did not study or know any German before I left, and I assumed I would just learn as I went. Not a good decision. I could hear the words around me, but I didn't know the "language." As I began to study the language, I began to pick up a word here and a word there. After more effort and study, I picked up a sentence here and there and began to speak a sentence occasionally. There was still much communication going on around me that I was missing, and I began to pick up some of it, but it took much more effort, study, and time before I could actually enter into a personal conversation with another person.

God has a language
Perhaps God has a language of his own, and it is up to us to learn it! Perhaps God's communication is happening all around us, and we miss it because we do not know the language of God.

A good biblical example of this is Samuel. You most likely remember this somewhat humorous story from the First Book of Samuel 3:1–10.

> During the time young Samuel was minister to the Lord under Eli, a revelation of the Lord was uncommon and vision infrequent. One day… Samuel was sleeping…The Lord called to Samuel, who answered, "Here I am." He ran to Eli and said, "Here I am. You called me." "I did not call you," Eli said, "Go back to sleep." So he went back to sleep. Again the Lord called Samuel, who rose and went to Eli. "Here I am," he said. "You called me." But he answered, "I did not call you, my son. Go back to sleep." At that time Samuel was not familiar with the Lord, because the Lord had not revealed anything to him yet. The Lord called to Samuel again, for the third time. Getting up and going to Eli, he said, "Here I am. You called me." Then Eli understood that the Lord was calling the youth. So he said to Samuel, "Go to sleep, and if you are called, reply, 'Speak, Lord, for your servant is listening.'"

There are several things to learn from this story. First, learning to hear God speak to us is a process; it takes time and experience. Both Eli and Samuel took a while to understand that God was speaking. "At that time Samuel was not familiar with the Lord." Samuel was new to this, to the ways of God and the language of God.

Almost everyone has the same ability to hear, but we all know that not everyone has the same skill at listening. Just as we learn how to be better at communication with humans, we must learn how to communicate with God. We learn the ways of God and how to listen and hear his voice speak to us.

I think the proper attitude to have in approaching this topic on hearing God speak is to avoid two extremes. The first extreme is to think that hearing God speak is an essentially impossible, highly mystical experience that is reserved for select holy people. When we think this way, we dismiss and pay almost no attention to God's communication in our life. People who think this way may grant that God has directed their life in some very general fashion, but daily life and our decisions are left up to us alone. Perhaps we even pray and offer our decisions up to God, but we do not expect God's response or direction regarding our decisions.

The second extreme is to take hearing God speak to us too lightly or flippantly, as if we have a direct line to God. Some people speak rather casually about God directing their lives and frequently say things like, "God told me to do this," or "The Lord wanted me to..." It is just not that simple.

Learning to hear God speak is very important, not only since it is critical to developing a healthy, dynamic relationship with God, but also because we have many questions in our lives for which we want God's help and direction. So how do we hear God speak?

⁓⑂⮡

PERSONAL REFLECTION

*What do you think and how do you feel
about God speaking to you?*

*Can you think of a time when you believe God was trying
to speak to you? What can you learn from this?*

CHAPTER TEN

A PRACTICAL GUIDE TO HEARING GOD

I propose seven areas of focus as you reflect on listening to God in a regular, daily fashion in your life. All seven areas need to be considered together because in most cases it is the union of two or more of these that makes for the most fruitful discernment.

Listening to God
1. Prayer: Prayer is consistent, daily communication with God
2. Intuition: An internal sense that God is talking to us
3. Scripture: God speaks to us through the words in the Bible
4. People: God speaks to us through people
5. Circumstances: God is present in all circumstances in our life and all of our life can speak God's voice to us
6. Reflection: God leads us in our life. Reflect on these times
7. Desire: We must want to hear God and be open to it

1. Prayer

As covered in the last chapter, there is simply no substitute for an ongoing, regular personal life of prayer. There are no shortcuts in the life of faith. Faith, like all relationships, is lived every day, and we grow in God's guidance of our lives by growing in our relationship with God in prayer. Prayer is itself the primary place where we develop our "intimacy" with God. Intimate communication, the opening and sharing of our mind and heart with the one who loves us, is where everything begins and where God's guidance is formed within us.

The guidance that is born of intimacy can be found in marriage as well. My wife and I are an example of this. Having been married for many years and working and growing in our communication for such a long time, Helen and I have come to pick up nonverbal communication from one another that is not present in our communication with other people. When we are at a party I can look across the room and see on her face, "It's time to go" or "This is fun; let's stay." Helen has not said a word, and no one else can see what her face is saying, but I can. This is the fruit of many, many years and much work at growing in communication in a daily way with one another.

Nourishing the capacity to receive God's guidance requires that growth in communication, sharing, and work as well. Specifically, God will communicate with us in daily prayer. When we yield and sit still in silence and open our mind and heart to God, often God will "speak." By *speak* I do not mean an audible voice, but a thought that comes to you, a sense of something in your mind or the experience of a presence with you, perhaps even moving your heart within with an emotion or intuition of the divine. This is a fruit of the Holy Spirit, when we experience God's love, peace, joy, or a sense of "being at home." This is often the communication of God to us. The opposite, not from God, would be distraction, confusion, or disturbance within.

How do you know if a thought you have in prayer is from God? Does it bring to you a new understanding or insight into yourself or God, or a question or struggle you are having? Does it carry with it the fruit of the Spirit mentioned above? If it does this thought may very well be God communicating with you.

Perhaps in prayer, in your openness to God, you recall a person or an event that happened in your life, and as you reflect on this person or event in prayer a new understanding or insight into that person or event comes to you. You understand the person in a new way, you interpret the event differently, and you may see for the first time that God was with you during an event that always seemed far from God. Again, this new understanding and insight brings with it a fruit of the Spirit. If the reflection on the past event is just disturbing or distracting, and you feel nothing of God's consolation, it most likely is a thought to let pass.

Perhaps an image comes to you in prayer. You just begin to imagine God's arms around you. You imagine God as your father or mother, or Jesus coming to you and smiling upon you as he embraces you. If this image brings with it a fruit of the Spirit, stay with it and "listen" to the image and let it "speak" to you.

There are many possibilities and ways in which God can communicate to us in personal prayer. This only happens if we are praying regularly, and the most important dimension that we bring to our prayer is "openness" or "listening." This is hard for us to do, and if we only listen for a few moments in our daily prayer, that is okay. It is as a disciple that we must practice to grow in our ability to hear God speak. Practice just "being" with God—not thinking or saying anything but just having an internal presence of being open to whatever God would give to you. One approach is to slowly repeat in your mind the words of Mary, "Let it be done to me according to your word."

2. Intuition

Intuition is an internal sense that we all have. For example, you meet someone for the first time and before the person even says anything you think to yourself, "trouble." Or you have the opposite reaction to someone you just meet: "This is a person I would like to get to know." When we look back on this initial encounter with the person, we often discover that our initial intuition revealed something to us that was very true about the person.

Intuition is not a feeling or an emotion. Intuition is a form of knowledge. "Knowing" in the Scriptures went beyond reason or rational knowing of the other. When the Bible speaks of "knowing," it means a form of knowing that is analogous to all the ways a man knows a woman and a woman knows a man; it is a complete knowing of the other. This knowing involves reason but also experience, emotion, intuition, physical knowledge, and a knowing born from profound intimacy with another.

Prayer is the way that an intimate "knowing" of God begins to grow within us. Just as we come to "know" another person through intimate communication, we come to know God through the intimate communication that happens when we pray.

As a way of understanding the mystery of the Trinity, theology has often spoken about the Holy Spirit as the love between the Father and the Son. This same intimate love that God the Father and God the Son have for one another is the very intimate love that has been given to us. When we grow in our relationship with the Holy Spirit, we are growing in an intimate, loving "knowledge" of God. We begin to intuit God's presence; we sense God's intimate movement and leadings in our life.

For example, you may have a sense that God is calling you to talk to a particular person, to reach out to them. It would be good to prayerfully listen to this sense. Does it stay with you? Are you feeling "moved" to do something you would not normally do? Do you experience a love or compassion for this person? Do you sense something going on in this person when you pray for them? All of this may be God leading you. After you have done your best in discernment, you act! If the encounter was God's will, the fruits of the Spirit are present. Or, when you consider reaching out to someone with whom you have a personal agenda at work, perhaps you realize after some reflection that you want to "straighten this person out" or "tell them the truth they need to hear." Perhaps you realize some emotions toward the person within you that are not based on charity or compassion for them. Then you are most likely not being led by God to reach out to this person.

I would like to share a personal experience that illustrates this well. Helen and I were visiting Assisi, the home of St. Francis. We were staying at a religious women's guest house that provided rooms and meals for visitors to Assisi. It was our last night there, and we were having dinner. Since it was the off-season there were only two other tables occupied that night, one by a large Italian family that was vacationing in Assisi and the other by a young woman who sat by herself drinking a glass of wine. The woman was quite attractive with long blond hair and blue eyes; she was dressed in a somewhat hip fashion, and had a steak of purple in her hair. As we ate dinner I began to have a sense, an intuition, that we should talk with this woman. The sense did not go away, and I felt it more and more. Now I had been married many years at that time, and I had made many mistakes in my marriage, but I was not foolish enough to suggest to my wife that we invite this young, attractive woman to join us for dinner. I also knew that my wife and I do not have much time together due to my ministry in the church, and that Helen understandably covets our time alone as a couple. So I silently offered a prayer to God.

If God wanted us to talk to this woman, God would have to tell Helen too. Sure enough, Helen began to look over to the young woman, again and again. Then she turned to me and said, "John, I think we should invite that woman over to have dinner with us." Well, if Helen suggested that, it must have been God! So we invited her over. What happened next was quite remarkable. She immediately opened up to us. She had just arrived from Sweden after a very long and difficult journey by train. She said she had come to Assisi on a spiritual quest, and although she was not a person of faith prior to this, she was now seriously seeking God. She had owned several stores and lived with a man for many years, but she had recently sold the stores, left the man, and come to Assisi. I will never forget her saying, "I am thirty years old, but I feel like I am fifty." Helen and I shared with her our journeys of faith, how we came to know God, and how our lives had changed. She listened attentively. After dinner I asked if she would like to continue the conversation. She agreed and we went to a room where, after some more talking, I asked if we could pray together. We prayed. Helen and I prayed out loud and the young woman silently. I will never forget the look in her eyes when we were finished. Something happened within her. We hugged as we said good-bye.

There are several elements to this story that are important. Both Helen and I had the same sense or intuition to invite the young woman over. This is one of the seven factors to consider in discernment—when other people are sensing the same thing you are, you can be more confident you are on the right track. Then we took a risk, which is part of the process. Most important was our reflection on the experience and how we saw the fruits of the spirit in the event. There was a clear touch of grace with us and in this woman's life. This example illustrates an important point in discernment and following the guidance of God that it is best when more than one way or function of discernment is present and all are pointing in the same direction before we act.

3. Bible

The Bible can be read for many different reasons, and all are good and valuable. A seeker reads the Bible to discover something about Christianity. A historian reads the Bible as a history book. Some read the Bible to discover the theology contained in the writings and the intent of the biblical authors. The Bible can also be read as a primary sourcebook for church doctrine, teaching, and catechesis. At the same time, the Bible can be read as a book written for "you." You might call the Bible God's personal love letter to you. When we read the Bible as a love letter, then the words of the Scriptures can come alive in a deeply personal, profound, and transformative way in our lives. The Bible becomes a primary way in which God will speak to you. This "hearing God speak" through the Scriptures would happen if we read a Scripture passage and asked not what this is saying about Christianity, the church, history, theology, or doctrine but instead what this passage is saying to me, to my life here and now. Seen this way, the Bible may very well speak to *you*.

This must be the case for us; otherwise why would the Bible play such a prominent role in Christianity and the gathering of the church on Sunday? In the Mass, there is a liturgy of the word and a liturgy of the Eucharist. Word and Eucharist together form one liturgy, one Mass, one sacrament. Catholics have been well formed to understand the Eucharist, the consecrated bread and wine, as the real Body and Blood of Christ. It is well understood that the reception of the Eucharistic bread and wine is a reception of Christ himself, a personal and communal "encounter of the risen Jesus." At the same time, Catholics often don't understand or appreciate the fullness of receiving Christ and encountering the risen Jesus through the word of God. It is during the liturgy of the word, through the reading of the Scriptures, meditating on the word and hearing the proclamation of the word in preaching that we are meant to have an encounter with, and a receiving of, Christ himself. No one puts this truth more profoundly and accurately than Origen, one of the fathers of the church, when he said this of sacred Scripture: "We should reverence every word of Scripture the same way we reverence every particle of the consecrated host." Catholics who believe in the real presence of the Body and Blood of Jesus in the Eucharist will well know the startling nature of Origin's words. This understanding would lead us to approach the Bible as a sacred word where God is "truly present" to us in our personal lives to communicate God's saving action. We would begin to discover the power of Scripture to speak to us a living and saving word. What do we do with every crumb of the host? We eat it! In the same way, we want every bit of the word of God to enter into us, to be absorbed into us—not just left on a shelf or heard and forgotten.

When you pray, try meditating on a Scripture passage. Perhaps an event in the life of Jesus comes to your mind in prayer. Enter the story; in your imagination, be a person in the event.

For example, you imagine yourself at the birth of Jesus. Imagine the animals, the hay, the smells, the people. What are you feeling? Perhaps you imagine you are a shepherd and Joseph asks you to hold the baby Jesus for a moment. What is that like for you? What is God saying to you?

Another example: perhaps you are experiencing a time of significant trial and suffering. You can imagine Mary going to the tomb and "weeping," and you join her in her tears, pouring out your heart to the one who loves you, waiting and looking at the tomb and seeing what happens.

When I was in college, I experienced an example of Scripture speaking to me as I prayed. I was in a chapel prayerfully reading the Bible, and I came across the passage when Jesus raises his friend Lazarus from the dead. The passage I was reading was this:

> When Mary came to where Jesus was and saw him, she fell
> at his feet and said to him, "Lord, if you had been here, my
> brother would not have died." When Jesus saw her weeping
> and the Jews who had come with her weeping, he became
> perturbed and deeply troubled, and said, "Where have you
> laid him?" They said to him, "Sir, come and see." Jesus wept. So
> the Jews said, "See how much he loved him." JOHN 11:32–36

As I was praying the thought came to my mind, "If something bad happened to me and Jesus was here, Jesus would weep for me, and those who saw his weeping would say, 'See how much he loved John.'" At this thought my eyes began to fill with tears. I was filled within by a new and deep experience of the love of Jesus for me that I had never considered before to this depth. This experience happened over forty years ago, and I still remember it.

Scripture passages can come into your life in unexpected ways and bring a surprise of grace. You hear a phrase at Mass, or read a verse that is hanging on a wall, or a passage may just come into your mind, and the words catch your attention. You most likely have heard these words many times before, but at this moment they connect with you and sometimes even directly with what you are going through at that particular time. You have a good idea this passage is God speaking to you because when you read or hear the words you know immediately that the words are speaking about your life. For example, you may have been hurt by someone and are feeling resentment, and you're not sure how to proceed with this emotion. The passage from Scripture comes to mind when Peter asks Jesus how many times we should forgive our neighbor, seven times? Jesus replies, "Not seven times but seventy times seven times." Forgiveness has now been entered into the struggle you are having, and it can be profoundly liberating.

4. People

The incarnation of God in Jesus, born as one of us, has profound implications. This means that all of humanity (and all of creation) is imbued with the divine. The very fact that God in Jesus became one of us is the most profound statement that God wants to communicate to us! God has gone to the greatest extent possible to communicate his saving love. The implications of this are wonderful and immense for us who believe in Jesus as the incarnation of the Son of God. There are many Bible passages that bear this out, yet one stands out with its radical clarity. Matthew 25:35–39: "When I was hungry you gave me food. I was thirsty and you gave me drink, a stranger and you welcomed me, naked and you clothed me, ill and you visited me." The response of both of the groups to whom these words were given is most telling. Both the ones who performed these acts of charity and those who did not had no idea it was Jesus with whom they were dealing. This one passage forcefully expresses the radical identification of Jesus with all of humanity, particularly the poor and vulnerable. In God's mind there is no separation. However, in our minds there is often a profound separation. How else can we explain our lack of consideration of other people as a primary source for God's communication and very presence in our midst?

People can communicate God to us at any time and in almost any circumstance. An act of charity, a smile, an encouraging word, or a statement of faith given to us during a time of trial can all be God speaking to us.

To keep our focus here on listening to God speak and direct our lives, I would like to give some recent examples in my own life of how other people are a primary source for God's communication to us.

Not long ago a member of our parish lost his wife to cancer. They were both very committed followers of Christ and members of our church. I was not able to attend the funeral, so the next time I saw the husband I went up to him and expressed my condolences. He is a very quiet man and rarely engages in any conversation. His response to me was given from a deep place within himself: "Part of life is leaving it. I know where she is." I was stopped by his words and could not respond. I had never heard such words of faith and acceptance from anyone at a time of such profound loss. I was caught up in a moment of God speaking to me of faith, hope, and surrender.

Not long ago, I went to visit my daughter and her two children. Her son, Theo, is four years old, and we are very close. At this visit Theo expressed his closeness and love for me in a way he never had up to this point. When I entered their house, Theo saw me from across the room and he said, "Pop-Pop" as he proceeded to run toward me and jump into my arms. Once there his body went limp in my embrace. At that moment, I thought of how we are to be with God, limp in the arms of his embrace. I was deeply touched by Theo's love and God's love.

These examples illustrate that God speaks to us all the time through other people. The limitation in hearing God speak is on our part. "When did we see you hungry?"

Another very helpful way to allow God to speak to us through other people is to directly seek out other people as partners with us in our journey of faith. There are several dimensions and ways that this can take place in our lives. You can choose to ask someone for specific spiritual direction. This is a committed meeting with someone with whom the nature of your meeting is to directly discuss how you are, or are not, hearing God lead and direct your life. This same discussion may happen more informally between friends and people whom you know at church.

The common thread in such discussions is about God's direction in our lives. When you consider someone to talk with, it is most important that you select people you trust and whose faith and discipleship you admire. A good way to proceed in this is to ask God in prayer to whom you should go for this. Then do it, and do it with some regularity if possible. Companionship on the journey of faith with a trusted guide is of utmost importance. St. Teresa of Ávila put it simply: "He who guides himself is a fool."

We did not baptize ourselves. Our faith and our Christian discipleship in many ways stand on the shoulders of the faith of other people. The reason this is so critical for our topic at hand is this: each of us can hear God wrongly. Together we are more likely to hear God correctly. St. John Neumann put it this way: "So much holiness is lost to the Church because brothers and sisters refuse to share the content of their hearts one with another." So much holiness, wholeness in our life of faith, is lost to us because we refuse to share our hearts and our faith journey with another.

During my preparation and study for the diaconate, I was required to have a spiritual director. I had hit a very low point in my journey. The time it required, the way the program was structured, the teachers—all felt like it was working against me, like it was a bad fit. I was seriously considering dropping out. I was meeting with my director and let this entirely spill out, and it wasn't pretty.

I was at a very dark place in my journey. After quietly listening to everything I said, my director, after a long silence, simply said one word, "Patience." Immediately the word fell into me. I knew deep within that God had spoken to me through my spiritual director. My racing mind was silenced, and my heart was beginning to be filled with a new trust and patience in God. That was it, one word. God spoke and I was free. I am not sure I would be in the ministry I am in today as a deacon without that one word.

5. Circumstances

If you are recently married, have children, are unemployed, or have had a death in your family, what are these circumstances in your life saying to you? What are the "signs of the times" in your life? Perhaps you just had a fight with your spouse, or a coworker did something unethical in your business, or you just made a lot of money in the stock market, or you were invited to become a member of a new ministry in your church. The circumstances of our lives are always with us, and our lives speak! What is important is that we listen. The most important question, one that we must ask over and over again, is this: "What is God saying to me in this?" It is very important for us to remember that in faith, there are no God-free zones. God is present in all of your life, and all of your life can speak God's voice to you. The most mundane and the most sublime aspects of our human lives are filled with the presence of God and are potential avenues of God's communication and direction for our lives.

It is best when the circumstances of our lives confirm or go along with something we have been sensing that God is saying to us in our personal prayer, or something we recently read in Scripture, or a suggestion from a friend that caught our attention.

For example:

1. You have been thinking that God is calling you to spend more time in regular prayer. Then the TV breaks or someone gives you a book on prayer they highly recommend or a series on prayer is offered at your church.

2. You have been thinking that God is calling you to be more generous with your money. Then you get a raise at work, or a Scripture passage comes to you on caring for the poor and avoiding greed, or someone you meet just happens to speak about how financial generosity in their life has become so freeing and liberating for them, or out of nowhere someone gives you a book on St. Francis that you read and feel inspired to live a greater simplicity of life.

3. You have been wondering what your gifts are or what your calling is to serve. Then you are invited to participate in a ministry that you have often thought may be a good fit for you, or a course comes to your church on "Living Your Strengths" that helps people discern their strengths and gifts for ministry, or you are having a conversation with someone who affirms you and says how they have always noticed a particular gift in you for ministry, or you hear a homily that calls us to step out of our comfort zones and serve others, and these words stir something within you.

Once again, it is better when more than one of these seven avenues for God's voice are woven together and saying essentially the same thing when we are considering God's direction in our lives. Having several avenues of God's voice speaking in unison helps us to interpret them correctly. It is very important to remember that we humans have a great proclivity to see what we want to see, and we can easily manipulate the process. We can be "sign happy" and substitute the hard work of real listening to avoid difficult decisions we don't want to make with signs we are all too eager to jump on because they say what we want to hear.

There's a funny story about this regarding a man who is just beginning a diet. He prays on his way to work that if there is no parking spot in front of the donut shop it will be a sign that God wants him to start the diet. On his tenth ride around the donut shop a parking spot finally opens up. He thanks God for another day before he begins the diet he knows he needs.

6. Reflection *What is a reflection of God in my life? his communication with me?*

Reflect on the times in your life when you believe you were genuinely led by God. What did you learn from this? Reflect on the times when you thought you were being led by God but later discovered you were not. What did you learn from this? Reflecting on these two questions, and learning from experience can be a source of much personal insight into God's speaking in your life.

Another way to consider reflection as an avenue of God's voice in your life is to simply reflect for a brief time each day on what God is saying to you that day. St. Ignatius of Loyola had a very simple formula that can be very helpful. Essentially, he suggests that at the end of each day we take time to reflect on the following: *When was I close to God today? When was I far from God today? What is God saying to me?* This is simple and can be very insightful.

God will speak through the moments of closeness to God and through the times of distance from God. Remember, there are no God-free zones. It is important to remember that these moments or aspects of our day need not be monumental but are most often very subtle. It may have been the way the morning sun reflected on your car windshield as you drove to work in the morning that caught your attention, and your mind pondered the beauty of the world. It may have been a genuine encounter with another person that reflected something of God to you. On the other hand, you were filled with anxiety during part of your day and were trying to control situations you cannot control. Perhaps you had feelings of loneliness and being misunderstood. What is God saying in the experiences of your daily life?

Whenever I would visit with my spiritual director, I would begin by letting out all the positive and negative aspects of my life at that time and all the ways I was graced by God and moved by God's presence and love, as well as all the struggles I was having with life, people, ministry, and sometimes prayer itself. My director would always say the same thing in response to me: "What is God saying to you in this?" At first, I found this very irritating. I would say to myself, "I don't know! That is why I am talking to you!" My director would just repeat the question.

After some time of entering into the discipline that my director was offering me, I began to get it. He was not there to tell me what God was saying to me. He was there to help me with the reflection and discovery that I had to find myself. Once we enter this reflection on a daily basis it becomes almost second nature and not arduous. We just rest in God's presence, in God's love for us, and reflect on what God is saying to us. Oftentimes it is not a word so much as an experience or a feeling: that I am loved, not alone, forgiven, empowered by the Holy Spirit, or called.

Often as we reflect on God's communication with us we are caught up in wonder that we even exist, that we have this life, that we even know and trust and have been so profoundly graced by this God who came to us in his Son, Jesus, and who has given us his Holy Spirit.

Remember, God is speaking all the time! Like radio waves bouncing around a room we are sitting in, God is there all the time. But we need to turn on the receiver and raise up the antenna. Try it; use the avenues God has given us to hear his words. Reflection on these avenues and how we are to consider all seven in a regular way in our lives is critical.

Paying attention to all the ways and avenues we have to hear God speak is very important to growing in our ability to better listen to God. Remember, listening is a life skill that some of us develop well and others do not, but we all can learn to listen to God. This need not be approached anxiously or with pressure to succeed but with a loving trust in God who longs to give us the Holy Spirit and guide our lives.

7. *Desire*

We must want it! God never forces himself on us, because that is not the nature of Love. Love must be free to be love. God seeks after us and is speaking to us all the time, but God will never force his will, or his word, upon us. As Augustine put it: "God will not save us without us." If we want to grow in our intimacy with God and become alive and fervent in God's divine love, and if we want God to direct our lives and reveal his will and ways to us, we must want it!

To seek and desire God and God's word is something we are actually called to as followers of Jesus. "Seek the Lord and he will be found. Call on him for he is near." This is expressed in the story of the unjust judge and the widow who wears the judge out by her incessant banging on his door for justice. The woman in this story has a passionate desire for justice and is moved to action by that desire. We are to be moved to prayer by the same passionate desire for what God loves when that love is within us as well. In effect, the gospel is saying, "Be like her!"

"If you, as sinful as you are, know how to give good things to your children, how much more will your heavenly Father send the Holy Spirit to those who ask?" (Luke 11:13). God wants to communicate with us and give us the power source for that communication to happen—the Holy Spirit. When we desire the very same thing that God wants to give to us, we are in a very good place in the journey of faith.

In short, ask, every day, for God to speak to you, as we hear in the Scriptures over and over: "Speak Lord, your servant is listening." "Let it be done to me according to your word." "Let it be your will O Lord, not mine."

Faith is expressed in desire; desire for God and God's will and direction in our lives. This is so important, for our resistance to God's direction and will is entrenched in our lives in very subtle and almost imperceptible ways. We all possess in a deep psychological and spiritual fashion what I like to call "filter systems." Essentially, we hear what we want to hear and filter out the rest.

An example of the filter system was provided for me by my children. The trash in the kitchen could be overflowing; I would raise my voice and say, "Who is going to take out the trash?" No one seemed to hear me. But if I offered ice cream everyone responded; they somehow "heard" this message and not the other.

This is not unlike what we do at a much more profound level in our lives of faith. Our abandonment to God is not complete, and our desires are distorted and at some level in conflict with one another. We desire God and God's will, but we also possess competing desires, such as:

- I want God only so much. I am not ready to abandon my lifestyle if God would ask me, so I don't open that area up to God in prayer and listening.
- I want to hear from God that God loves me and that I will live forever, but I don't want to hear about forgiveness,

because I have much anger toward someone who hurt me, and that person does not deserve to be forgiven.

- At some deep level, I do not trust God, because I think if I really trust God and am completely open that God will call me to something that will make me miserable. He will want me to give all my money to the poor or become a missionary, and I am just not cut out for that.

- I am afraid to fully trust God, because I have trusted someone and been seriously hurt, and I never want to take that risk again.

- My father or mother abused me or failed me in some significant way, and I believe in God, but not as one I can trust as a child does a loving parent.

- I am afraid that God is constantly waiting to condemn me for the things I have done in my life, and so I don't want to open myself to hearing what God has to say to me.

All of these deeply rooted psychological and spiritual issues keep us from fully desiring God. We live with our filter systems well in place, and we let them control our discipleship at a very deep level. Addressing this is at the very heart of what conversion means— "to have a new mind," to see God, self, life, and faith differently, the way God sees it. As we become converted, we trust, desire, and listen to God in new ways with an ever-greater amount of freedom, peace, and abandonment. God loves us with a passionate love that wants all of who we are, not just parts. God's love will not settle till we are in complete union with him. What we can do is be honest with ourselves and with God. We can bring our filter systems to God in prayer and offer our fears and mistrust and distorted thinking to God, our Father, who sees everything that is in secret and who loves us. We have nothing to fear. As we grow in abandonment to God and in desiring God and his call alone, we begin to hear God's voice more and more, his gentle, sweet, loving voice calling out to us to trust him.

A nice way to help this process when we pray is to slow down the mind. (There are many books that can help with how to do this.) Essentially, we want to acknowledge that we often listen to God, as we do to others, "with the motor running." Have you ever found yourself listening to other people when all the while you are thinking about what you are going to say as soon as they stop speaking? Sometimes you even interrupt them, because you see what you are thinking as so important for them to hear. This is not true listening. Listening desires to hear what the other has to say.

To enter into another's experience and thought is to walk in their shoes. When you are in the presence of a good listener, you know it. You feel listened to; you feel loved. True listening is a high form of loving the other. Listening to God is a high form of loving God. There are no short-cuts here, and there is no substitute for real listening—to being open to whatever God will say, to do your best to hear whatever that is, trusting—even if you do not like or want to hear his word in the beginning—that his word will bring you life. If it is forgiveness and you are still angry and resentful, then that is okay. Praying with the anger and resentment, bringing it to God in prayer, is much more authentic than pretending it does not exist or living in fear of facing it. "Okay, God, let it be done to me according to your loving will for me."

Main point
The main point in considering how God speaks to us is considering how all of the above are working together to make guidance possible. Healthy discernment is listening to all of these

ways that God speaks. It is best when more than one of the above are saying the same thing or pointing in the same direction. A good analogy is the fibers of a rope. When you cut a strong rope, you discover that the rope is made of many very thin fibers. It is the weaving together of these tiny fibers that makes the rope so strong. An individual fiber can easily be broken, but once it is woven together with other fibers, it becomes very strong. This is how healthy and confident guidance can be brought about in our lives—not taking certain indications of God's voice in isolation from other avenues of God's voice. The bigger the decision, the more we should want more of the above avenues essentially saying the same thing in a greater depth.

Finally, we *act*! In action, we then discover more discernment. The fruits of the action will speak to us with great clarity about how well we have heard the voice of God. If we are humble and are willing to learn from our mistakes, if our intentions are good with a heart that is genuinely seeking God, and if we do our discernment within the context of a community, we have nothing to fear. All will be well. Just do your best. God loves you.

⇥⇤

PERSONAL REFLECTION

Reflect on the seven ways God speaks to you.
What was new? What did you learn?

What would you do differently now in listening
to God speak to you?

CHAPTER ELEVEN

PRAYER: LOVE AND PRESENCE

Prayer consists not in thinking much,
but in loving much.   TERESA OF ÁVILA

The above statement from Teresa of Ávila reflects the call of disciples to love God at all times and in every circumstance and to know that God's love for us is at the very heart of faith. This love of God is not a pious sentimentality but a living presence that can penetrate every circumstance of our lives.

Loving God: A testimony

I know of no better illustration of this than the writings and life of Cardinal Francis Xavier Nguyen Van Thuan of Vietnam in his book *Testimony of Hope*. In 1975, Bishop Francis was arrested and spent the next thirteen years in prison, nine of which were in solitary confinement. He lived in a cell without windows, in total darkness, in suffocating heat and humidity that drove him to the point of insanity. However, his greatest torment was that he was forced to abandon his diocese. He writes:

> I could not sleep because I was so tormented by the thought of being forced to abandon my diocese, and of the many works that I had begun for God now going to ruin. I experienced a kind of revolt in my whole being. One night, from the depths of my heart, a voice said to me, "Why do you torment yourself like this? You must distinguish between God and the works of God....[There] are works of God, but they are not God! If God wants you to leave all of these works, do it right away and have faith in him! You have chosen God alone, not his works!"
>
> This light gave me a new peace and completely changed my way of thinking. It helped me to surmount moments that were almost physically impossible to overcome. From then on, a new strength filled my heart that stayed with me for thirteen years. Feeling my human weakness, I renewed my choice of God in the face of very difficult situations, and I was never without peace.
>
> To choose God and not the works of God. This is the foundation of the Christian life in every age. PP. 42–3

What a testimony to the power of faith to choose God alone— to love God in every circumstance (even in a stinking, dark jail cell), and to experience the peace that comes from knowing the love of God. As important as our love and service are to others, as a direct expression of our love for God, there remains the nature of love that is *presence*. To love God from our heart and to choose God before all else, even other very good things, is to live the commandment to "love God with all your heart, your being, your mind and your strength." This is the one thing that is necessary and is to be brought into every circumstance and moment of your life. Taking this approach to faith into our daily lives will bear dramatic fruit, and we will grow in vibrant faith. Knowing that we are always with God, always loved by God, and always loving God changes our lives, and we begin to live our life of faith more fully, deeply, and richly.

Living in the present

Living our life of faith more fully enables us to begin to live more and more in the present moment each day of our lives. How rich it is to live in the present moment, which is actually the only moment we have. Living in the present is critical for the life of faith, and it is very difficult for us to do. We spend most of our time worrying about the future and regretting our past mistakes. There is value in reflecting back and looking forward, but the problem is that the past and the future do not reflect the present. The past is over and the future is not here yet. C.S. Lewis illustrates this well in his book *The Screwtape Letters*. The book is the correspondence between two devils, a senior devil and an apprentice devil. The senior devil is mentoring the apprentice devil on how to attack and lead the man he has been assigned to away from God. At one point the senior devil gives the following advice to his apprentice.

> Get the human to think about the past...Get him to think about the future...but in all cases, keep him from thinking and living in the present. Because that is the only place where he can meet our enemy [God].

We can only meet God in the present. Bishop Francis discovered this, even in the worst of conditions, and he discovered God's peace. We do this by practicing God's presence and living in the present moment, loving God, and being loved by God. How rich our life would be to know that every moment we are loved! How would we pray throughout our day? Where would our thoughts go? How would we view a sunrise or a sunset? What would we say to people we love, and how would we deal with our resentments?

In Greek, there are two words for "time": *chronos* and *kairos*. *Chronos* is the time on a clock. *Kairos* is the important time, the time with meaning, like the time you fell in love, gave birth to a child, lost a loved one, or when you knew what you wanted to do with your life. This is a time that stays with you. These events are part of you and are with you always. The resurrection of Jesus is a *kairos* event. It is with us always, and as we grow in union with Christ, it becomes more and more a part of who we are. This is no small thing. The first words that Jesus speaks in Mark's gospel (the earliest written gospel) are these: "This is the time of fulfillment. The kingdom of God is at hand. Repent, and believe in the gospel." The "time" Jesus is using is *kairos* time. The time of Jesus' coming is a *kairos* time, an important time, like no other, that is with us always! To "repent" in Greek is to have a new mind and to think new and differently than before. In this Scripture, it is a call to think and see the one who has come and is with us. Jesus' coming is now!

This coming of Jesus is with us at all times, and when we practice living in the present we move from seeing prayer and our connection with God as something for our private time, to recognizing a God with whom we are connected *all* the time. I believe faith is like being in love. When we really love another, we love the person all the time. The nature of love is not to be contained, limited, controlled, regulated, or parceled out. By its very nature, love is all encompassing; love spills out. If married couples only think of their partner or communicate with one another for twenty minutes after dinner, while admirable and valuable, it would not be enough. It would not reflect the nature of love. Similarly, if someone goes to church once a week and that is their only conversation with God, then the relationship will suffer. When you love someone, you often think about that person; they are like the background in your life—always there with you somehow.

A nice illustration of this kind of love is found in the movie *Forrest Gump*. Forrest is deeply in love with a woman named Jenny. He is separated from her for several years, and during that time he runs across the country. After they are reunited Forrest recounts his travels to Jenny. He speaks of all the things he saw, the people he met, the beauty of the nature that surrounded much of his adventure. Afterward Jenny says to Forrest, "Oh, Forrest, I wish I was there." To which Forrest replied, "You were." Fervent disciples, like those in love, carry the beloved everywhere they go and are never separated.

Practical tips

Married people naturally have many practical things in their lives that remind them of the other person and help to generate ongoing love for one another. Married people wear wedding and engagement rings. They carry pictures of their spouse or children on their phone, in their wallet or purse, and often have pictures on their desk at work or in their home. These images are reminders of the ones we love, and they help us to stay connected. A multitude of seemingly small actions can have a significant positive effect on the relationship we have with those we love. The examples are many: the spontaneous phone call or email just to say hi, the surprise of a nice dinner or flowers, leaving a little note, sending cards and gifts, playing a special song, wearing the shirt or dress the other likes, and spontaneous affection. The list goes on and on. All of these seem rather insignificant in themselves, but they all have an effect and bring life and vibrancy into a relationship.

Spontaneous prayer

One means of practicing God's presence is saying brief words of prayer throughout the day—whatever one spontaneously wants to say to God. In the Eastern Christian tradition, the "Jesus Prayer" was developed as a short prayer to be prayed spontaneously throughout the day in a repetitive fashion. The traditional Jesus prayer goes like this: "Lord Jesus, have mercy on me a sinner." One could say any variation of this prayer. One that I often pray comes from Psalm 33: "Lord, let your mercy be on me as I place my trust in you." When I pray this way, I do not think my prayer is making God have mercy on me, but I see this prayer as a way of opening myself to the mercy of God that is always mine, always given to me, and with me at every moment of my life. It is a prayer that creates receptivity to God in our hearts and minds. Sometimes, when I go into a difficult meeting or when I am counseling someone who is in great anguish and has very complicated problems, I often pray to myself the name of Jesus. I just pray, "Jesus, Jesus, and Jesus." This calms me and opens me to the direction of the Holy Spirit as I try to minister to another.

A powerful example of this kind of prayer is found in the book *Flags of Our Fathers*. In this book we hear about the life of John Bradley, who was one of the flag raisers on Iwo Jima. John Bradley was a medic during the battle and would move from one horribly mangled soldier to another trying to give medical assistance. What he witnessed on Iwo Jima was horrific. As he went through the battle day after day, he would continually pray to himself, "Blessed Mother, help us." Bradley would pray this simple prayer over and over and over. This prayer sustained him through the battle and empowered him to acts of bravery and self-sacrifice. After the war, he would say this same prayer every night before bed. One night his wife asked him what he was praying. After he told her she too joined him in this prayer every night. "Blessed Mother, help us." Today, chiseled on John Bradley's simple gray headstone are the words: "Blessed Mother, help us."

Symbols

Symbols can be powerful reminders of our faith, such as a cross on the wall, the fish symbol for Jesus, or a Bible on a table. For many Catholics, it is simply carrying a rosary in their pocket or a statue of a saint that inspires them in their discipleship. St. Pope John Paul II would inscribe on the top of all the papers he wrote the letters "AMDG." This stands for a Latin phrase that means "For the greater glory of God." This was his reminder of why he did all that he did in his life. During the persecution of the Irish people when the English forced them to renounce their Catholicism, the faithful Irish created a crucifix that was just small enough and narrow enough to slip under the sleeve of their shirt. They could hold the crucifix when the English were not around and simply slide it under their sleeve when they came by. They would have been in big trouble if the crucifix were discovered, so it must have had a significantly powerful symbolic effect on their faith for them to risk this.

Other faith traditions do this as well. I was in a men's locker room after a workout at a gym when a man came in dressed like most other people, with a baseball cap and jacket. When he took off the cap I saw a yarmulke on his head. When he took off his jacket I saw a prayer shawl under his shirt. On the doorway of a Jewish home is a mezuzah, which is a small object that contains a fragment of the Jewish Scriptures. Jews touch this as they enter their home. All such symbols bring to mind what we want and need to remember throughout our day. It is how we keep in touch with what is important to us and whom we love.

A technology fast

We live in a world of noise now more than ever. To have any sense of prayer in our life will require a direct and concerted effort to develop silence in some form. I like to call it "fasting from noise." Christians sometimes fast from good things, like food, to intensify their prayer. Today, more than ever, Christians need to fast from other good things—all the noise, information, and stimulation that is bombarding us in an endless fashion. Simple things like turning off the radio, computer, tablet, or smartphone can be a wonderful way to be with God and turn our thoughts to him. Deciding not to watch television on certain nights and to experience the quiet of the evening or forcing ourselves not to look at our phones as soon as we wake up in the morning are ways of cultivating silence. Silence will have a dramatic effect on our life of prayer and practicing the presence of God, and this is no small thing, especially in our modern day.

In his wonderful book *The Gift of Rest*, former Senator Joe Lieberman reflects on the importance of the Sabbath day in the life of Jewish faith and says the following about the challenges of our modern day:

> Every generation has its own pharaoh and its own slave masters, uniquely based on the culture of the time. Our pharaoh may be electronic devices—computers, televisions, iPhones—that mesmerize us, dominating hour after hour of our lives. Even when we think we are at leisure, they invade our attention, holding us in their grip and separating us from our family and friends—sometimes from our faith.

Music...Nature

I remember hearing the results of a survey that asked, "What is the context in which you most often have had a religious experience?" The most frequent answer was nature, and the second most frequent was being in the presence of great religious music. This begs three questions: Where do nature and religious music figure into our lives? Where do we pray best? What effect does certain religious music have on our life of prayer? Walking and being outside in nature has a wonderfully prayerful effect on me. Sometimes a song at church can catch me and convey such a powerful feeling of the love of God. Many people say the same; so we need to cultivate nature and music in our lives as a way of cultivating prayer.

A special place

For some of us, it is a church or a special place that draws us to prayer. Serving in a soup kitchen and serving homeless people can draw us into prayer. When I was young my father would sometimes take me to work with him in Manhattan, and each time we would begin the day with a visit to St. Patrick's Cathedral. Even when I was young the cathedral had an impact on me. I was drawn out of myself into a different space. Whenever I go to New York City now, I always visit St. Patrick's and still experience the effect it has on me.

Quotes

Special quotes or sayings can also have an effect upon us. Words can be powerful communicators of God, and certain phrases can catch us in very special ways. I remember going to the office of a friend who had on her wall a picture frame around a broken mirror so that when you looked at the mirror you saw your reflection, but your face was broken up. The following words were inscribed beneath the framed broken mirror: "Broken though we are, we are still reflections of the one who loves us." I was so taken with that image and the saying beneath it that I have never forgotten them and offered them to so many hurting people who have found comfort and inspiration in those words.

Gestures

An interesting gesture made by St. Ignatius of Loyola demonstrates how practical actions can help us continue in God's presence. The tale has been told among the Jesuit community that before Ignatius would enter a room for a meeting with others he would slap the frame of the door as he entered. The sound would get everyone's attention and would help Ignatius bring to mind the presence of the Holy Spirit as he entered and began the meeting. The sound and the gesture were a reminder for Ignatius, and such simple acts as blessing ourselves, nodding our heads, bowing, kneeling, raising arms and hands to God can all do the same. These gestures do not need an explanation but are spontaneous actions of the heart. These spontaneous gestures are what people in love do toward the one they love.

Art

Religious art is another avenue for invoking God's presence. Religious art has been with us from the very beginning of Christianity. In the catacombs we find the earliest depictions of Christ. One is Jesus as a young man with his arms outstretched. The second is Jesus as a young shepherd with a lamb over his shoulders. Here Jesus is young and vibrant and the good shepherd who seeks out and saves the lost. This is the Jesus of the early church, a church that wanted to remember this Jesus through painting his image on the wall of an underground cemetery—a place of death that is, in faith, a place of life.

There is something about art that draws us into another reality and affects our minds and hearts in a way that words do not. I remember the first time I was in Rome and saw Michelangelo's *Pietà*. As soon as I looked up I was stopped in my tracks. My mind went blank, and I was captivated by the sculpture. I felt as if I was being drawn into the death of Jesus and the person of Mary in a new way, as if I was there. It left a deep impression, and the experience I had of Jesus' death is hard to explain. I felt a new understanding of this event and the person of Mary. I remember Mary's broad shoulders and the limp and lifeless body of Jesus draped in her outstretched arms.

Religious art in our lives is a powerful and ever-present aid in living in God's presence. In my office I have a copy of the cross that spoke to St. Francis, "Rebuild my Church." I also have a picture of Michelangelo's creation scene in the Sistine Chapel with just the two hands of God the Father and Adam almost touching. These images have an effect on me and remind me of how God still speaks to us and how God, in Jesus, still tenderly creates and loves his creation.

The purpose for practicing God's presence is well expressed by Ronald Rolheiser when he writes in *Sacred Fire*:

> To "pray always" invites us, rather, to live our lives against a certain horizon. It does not necessarily mean to stop work and go to formal prayer, important though that is at times. The point is that we need to do everything within the context of a certain awareness, like a married man who goes on a business trip and who, in the midst of a demanding schedule of meetings and social engagements, is somehow always anchored in a certain consciousness that he has a spouse and children at home. Despite distance and various preoccupations, he knows that he is "married always." That awareness, more than the occasional explicit phone call home, is what keeps him anchored in this most important relationship. Our relationship with God is the same. We need to "pray always" by doing everything out of that kind of awareness.

What we are doing here in all these simple, even ordinary, actions is to create within ourselves the ability to be present to the one who is always present to us. God's primary voice to us is not words but presence—the presence of love. When I am with my young grandchildren I see, understand, and experience this so wonderfully. Because my grandchildren are three and four years old, our conversations are not filled with much profound thinking or analysis, and yet we are always in conversation through the presence we share and their full presence in each moment. When I am with my grandchildren I don't think about other things. I am fully caught up in their movement, wonder, activity, and way of being that is so fully present to me: When we are living in the present we discover that kind of wonder, joy, and love.

Fervent disciples who live in the present are playful and wonder-filled. It is fun to be a fervent disciple!

⇥⇤

PERSONAL REFLECTION

How does the idea of
"living in the present" speak to you?

....

What helps you the most now,
and what would you like to add to your life
to better live in the present?

CHAPTER TWELVE

SERVICE

*The most potent and acceptable prayer is the prayer that leaves
the best effects...those that are followed up by actions.*

TERESA OF ÁVILA

Prayer in action

> [One day Jesus was asked,] "Which commandment in the
> law is the greatest?" Jesus replied, "You shall love the Lord,
> your God, with all your heart, with all your soul, and with
> all your mind. This is the greatest commandment and the
> first commandment. The second is: You shall love your
> neighbor as yourself." MATTHEW 22:36–39

Jesus was asked for the one greatest commandment, but Jesus
responded with two commandments, not one. However, for Jesus
the two *are* one. In the gospels it is clear that for Jesus there is no
separation in our love for God and our love for our neighbor. It
is like two sides of the same coin. A coin has two sides, not one,
and yet it is one coin.

I am often surprised by how some books on prayer do not mention the life of service, charity, and love of neighbor. If prayer and faith are seen as disconnected from our way of living toward others, we will breed a dysfunctional and dangerous spirituality. "If anyone loves me, he or she will keep my commandments" (John 14:15). Prayer, faith, and our love for God are expressed and lived in our service and love of our neighbor. Our service and love of our neighbor are also ways of loving God. In any healthy relationship, each partner discovers the love of the other not only through their communication with one another but through the actions of the other toward them. Love is as love does. Aristotle said: "Don't listen to what people say, watch what people do." St. Cyril of Jerusalem put it this way: "Our actions have a tongue of their own; they have an eloquence of their own, even when the tongue is silent. For deeds prove the lover more than words."

All the time…All people

Discipleship is "all the time" and encompasses everything in our lives—all our words, actions, thoughts, and emotional responses, how we use our time, talent, and money, everything! God loves us at "every moment of our existence," and our response to that love is at every moment of our existence. As Paul says, "In him we live and move and have our being." Because we have received mercy, we live in that mercy toward all.

The gospel is replete with the words of Jesus and, story after story, driving home that our actions towards others are in fact our actions toward God. Perhaps no other parable has come to define the importance and essential need for encountering Jesus in the service we offer to another person than the separation of the sheep and the goats.

"I was hungry and you gave me food, I was thirsty and you gave me drink, a stranger and you welcomed me, naked and you clothed me, ill and you cared for me, in prison and you visited me." MATTHEW 25:35–36

God identifies himself so intimately with the hungry, the thirsty, the stranger, the naked, the sick, and those in prison that there is no separation here between God and those who suffer in these ways. What is most chilling about this parable is that it is a judgment scene. Here, all the nations are assembled before the king of creation, and these are the words they will hear; in these words the judgment is made.

During my life I have been asked many times, by a variety of Christian people, about my salvation. "Are you saved?" "Are you born again?" "Have you given your life to Jesus Christ?" "Are you a believer?" "Are you receiving sacraments regularly in your life?" "Are you living in a state of grace?" However, I have never heard, "Are you living Matthew 25?" Am I living these very words of Jesus? I believe Matthew 25 must be God's revealed word, since humans would never have thought this up as the judgment of their lives. Here, we are not judged by our "right belief," our intellectual convictions, creative ability, social status, achievement, or society's judgment about us. No, in the parable we are judged by love and mercy, concretely expressed in our love, mercy, and care for others.

In this gospel passage Jesus addressed two groups: those who showed mercy and care for others and those who did not. What is remarkable is that neither group saw God in the suffering ones. Both groups completely missed Jesus' identification with the suffering, and yet both received the same reply from Jesus making that identification utterly clear: *Amen, I say to you, what you did or did not do for one of the least brothers and sisters of mine, you did or did not do for me.* The shock of the parable is that it was *Jesus*!

Fr. Geah, a missionary who lived and served in Haiti for forty-two years, said the following words in a homily he gave on this parable, words that I will never forget: "The distance we keep from the poor is the distance that God keeps from us."

Works of mercy

The *Catechism* defines "works of mercy" as follows:

> *Works of mercy* are charitable actions by which we come to the aid of our neighbor in his spiritual and bodily necessities. Instructing, advising, consoling, comforting are spiritual works of mercy, as are forgiving and bearing wrongs patiently. The corporal works of mercy consist especially in feeding the hungry, sheltering the homeless, clothing the naked, visiting the sick and imprisoned, and burying the dead. Among all these, giving alms to the poor is one of the chief witnesses to fraternal charity: it is also a work of justice pleasing to God. (**2447**)

Social activist Dorothy Day put it best when she said, "Everything a baptized person does every day should be directly or indirectly related to the Corporal and Spiritual Works of Mercy."

In personal prayer we encounter the risen Jesus and God's love for us, and we are changed by that love. When we serve another in love we also encounter the risen Jesus and God's love for us, and we are transformed.

The following image speaks of how this works out in our life of discipleship and prayer. We can imagine our early stages in prayer like someone who prays with their arms up, outstretched to God—a very nice way to pray. However, as we grow in the limitless, fathomless, all embracing love of God, our experience of this divine love gradually lowers our arms till they are out before us, open to embrace all whom we meet. When our arms are outstretched to God and to others at the same time, then we are in prayer recognizing that there is no separation in our love of God and our love of our neighbor.

Johnny Cash was once asked why he performed concerts in prisons. His reply was, "Because the gospel tells me to." Johnny Cash got it. Discipleship is about living the love commandment—doing what we are called to do not because we feel like it but because Jesus said it.

When you love someone, you trust that person and you trust what they say to you. You believe too that they want what is best for you. Disciples who love God are those who trust God. They trust that God's word and ways are best for them and for this world, and they act on them. Vibrant faith comes from vibrant love and from vibrant living of that faith and love of God. When we love God, we love one another and when we love one another we love God. In doing this our love and faith grow, love "happens" within us and among us. We discover greater and greater capacity for loving. Prayer and love are meant to have an effect on us and how we live. Again, St. Teresa of Ávila: "The most potent and acceptable prayer is the prayer that leaves the best effects... those that are followed up by actions." When we act on our prayer, on the callings we perceive in our prayer, and on the word of God, our prayer is complete. Without the response or the action, the grace given in prayer is never fully received and actualized in our lives. Of course, we will stumble along the way, always striving not for spiritual perfection but for spiritual progress.

Consider the parable of a man who had two sons. To the first he said: "Son, go and work in the vineyard today." The son replied, "I will not." But afterwards, he changed his mind and went. The second son replied, "Yes, sir." But he did not go. Which did the Father's will? The first! The one who eventually acted even though he initially said no.

When we continue to experience a personal encounter with Jesus Christ, it is meant to be life-changing, with lasting repercussions. Encountering the risen Jesus and God's love for us is not in isolation from the rest of our lives. We experience mercy and forgiveness, and then we respond by becoming merciful and forgiving. When we experience the love and care of God, we become loving and caring of others. However, if we are not open to the actions of God in our lives, then we may miss the opportunity for growth that God has given us. We may write it off as a lucky turn of events instead of the miracle that it was, and we miss the conversion God has offered us.

When two people fall in love it is a wonderful experience, but that experience will not fully impact their lives if the two people do not recognize the opportunity to live lives of service, care, and commitment to each other. Because we are loved by God, we should naturally respond in love of others. If we are forgiven by God, we respond in forgiveness of others. This is how the love and mercy of God comes more and more alive within us. Gandhi put it this way: "Happiness is when what you think, what you say, and what you do, are in Harmony." This can also be called integrity, congruency, discipleship, and holiness.

Being with Jesus

When someone new came to Mother Teresa's mission she would say to them, "You are not here to work, you are here to be with Jesus." Now anyone who has witnessed her community in action knows how extremely hard they work, and yet they see no separation between their work and being with Jesus. This is a healthy and vibrant spirituality and life of prayer.

This is hard for us to grasp and even harder for us to live. Being with Jesus in all aspects of our life is challenging, difficult, and sets us apart.

When my son, Michael, was in college he was studying finance and received an internship with Goldman Sachs. This was a great opportunity for him with the top financial firm in the world. One day Michael told me that he had entered the cafeteria for lunch and had seen that all the seats were occupied except for one table in the corner where the kitchen employees were sitting. The kitchen employees were mostly black or Hispanic and dressed in the uniforms of their work. Michael said that he hesitated for a moment but then sat down at their table for lunch, and he told us that he had a great time and wonderful conversation. To be honest, my first thought upon hearing this was, "That is not good for his career." Then I caught myself and thought, "Well, that is how we raised him." Then I realized that if the company didn't want him because he sat with the kitchen employees at lunch, then it was not the right company for him. My initial thought was simply not consistent with the gospel, and it took me a moment to recover. The life of a fervent disciple of Christ creates a formation in a new self-understanding—to see yourself as God sees you and to live as a reflection of who you are.

Who we are and how we are to live is poignantly captured in the words of Teresa of Ávila:

> Christ has no body now but yours, no hands but yours, no feet but yours. Yours are the eyes through which Christ's compassion must look out on the world. Yours are the feet with which He is to go about doing good. Yours are the hands with which He is to bless us now.

PERSONAL REFLECTION

Reflect on a time when your service to another was an encounter with Jesus.

Reflect on service and ministry as an extension of your prayer and faith. How does this speak to you? How does this challenge you?

CHAPTER THIRTEEN

COMMUNITY

*Jesus turned and saw them following him and said to them,
"What are you looking for?" They said to him, "Rabbi, where are
you staying?" He said to them, "Come, and you will see."
So they went and saw where Jesus was staying, and they
stayed with him that day.* JOHN 1:38–39

A shared life

So far, I've been talking about what we can do as individual people of faith. But the bottom line is living a life of faith is seldom done on your own, as an individual. The world around us is just so big and so challenging, and life is so complex and difficult, that growing in faith without some support is difficult to unlikely. Community is the context in which fervent faith best develops and is sustained in the life of a disciple of Jesus.

Once again, the analogy of the life of faith is that of a seed planted in the soil. The seed grows and develops outside of our control. The life of the seed is within itself and comes forth as a gift, and so it is with the life of God that is given as a gift, planted within us as a grace freely given. At the same time the seed planted in the soil best develops and grows under certain conditions. The seed requires regular water, sunlight, and fertilizer. Once surrounded by these conditions the seed grows steadily and fruitfully. It is the same with the vibrant life of faith. The conditions of prayer, service, and community need to nourish the life of the disciple in a regular, ongoing way for that life of faith to grow and become fervent.

I have specifically avoided using the word "church" for several reasons. A discussion of church and what it means in the life of faith is a very large topic and would move beyond the focus of this book. Another reason is that the word itself brings to mind many different understandings of the meaning and purpose of church. When someone hears the word "church," what is often brought to mind is a building, an institution, a denomination, clergy, doctrine, and who is right/wrong in following the message of Jesus Christ. While these dimensions are all very important, I would like us to focus on the word "community." – not church

Community may in fact be a dimension of someone's experience of church, but often community is not what one has come to know church to be for them. This is another reason why community is my focus here. The importance of community cuts across denominational lines and is often missed, or not present, in the life of people of faith who go to church. The critical and vital dimension community plays in the life of fervent faith is often not even considered in our contemporary, postmodern world—a world in which many believers in Jesus would call themselves spiritual but not religious. What they may mean is that they have faith in Jesus but avoid any regular contact with a community of believers because they associate the community of believers with church and all the religious baggage that word implies. This way of thinking is extremely prevalent and one of the main reasons for the lack of fervency in people of faith today.

Let us take a look at why the role of community is so very important in the life of the fervent disciple.

We cannot do faith alone

There are two things we cannot do alone in this life: marriage and Christian faith. We did not baptize ourselves, and someone during our life spoke the name of Jesus to us. We all stand on the shoulders of people of faith in our life today and on the shoulders of people of faith who have gone before us. "Since we are surrounded by so great a cloud of witnesses, let us rid ourselves of every burden and sin that clings to us and persevere in running the race that lies before us while keeping our eyes fixed on Jesus" (Hebrews 12:1–2). Now that is a statement of fervent faith that is clearly connected with the community of faith that surrounds us!

Christian community in its truest form is simply the "gathering of people of faith." This is not just any gathering; it is a purposeful and shared gathering. The purpose of this community is life with and in the risen Jesus and living in the power of the Holy Spirit so that we can become fervent disciples who engage in a common mission. The sharing of this community is the sharing of human life with all its complexities, sorrows, and joys, and the shared life of service together for one another and the world.

Over and over in the Bible, we see the deep importance of this "gathering and sharing" of the people of faith. Consider the context in which the Holy Spirit, the power source for the vibrant life of faith, came to the first believers. The Holy Spirit came when they were "gathered together in prayer." It was when the believers were doing what Jesus told them to do, "gather together," a gathering of shared weakness and human failure and also a gathering of prayer into which the Holy Spirit came. Mary is there praying with them. The one who received the incarnation of Jesus in private is now receiving the coming of the Holy Spirit and the "birth" of the church in the context of community. (One might call this the second "incarnation" of God among us.) The Holy Spirit best comes today in the same context, when we are "gathered together" in prayer, asking the Holy Spirit to come. There is no end to this. Mary had received the Holy Spirit during the incarnation, and she is praying with the community asking for more of the Holy Spirit. Together, gathered in prayer, they ask over and over for the Holy Spirit to come. These are clearly fervent disciples!

In John's gospel the center of fervent faith came with the experience of the risen Jesus, who also "breathed" on the disciples the Holy Spirit. Again, the context was the same. It was the gathering of the disciples, even in fear and failure, which was the context in which the risen Jesus came and gave the gift of the Holy Spirit. It was in this gathering that Jesus appeared in their midst and they encountered the risen one.

Thomas was not present at the gathering and did not meet the risen Jesus. The biblical author is making a statement here: "Not good Thomas, not good!" The disciple needs to be with the community in order to meet the risen Christ. In fact, it is only when Thomas rejoins the community that he meets the risen Jesus. It is the same today. If we want to meet the risen Christ and receive the Holy Spirit, we see that the best context for this to happen is community—the gathering and sharing of life and faith.

Conversing and debating

In Luke's gospel we discover this eloquently expressed in the story of the road to Emmaus. Luke is attempting to answer the question the early Christians were beginning to ask, "Where is the risen Jesus found?" Luke gives three places where the risen Jesus is found in this story. The first two are familiar enough to us: the Eucharist and the Scriptures. The third, however, is often missed by the modern reader. It is community. Here we have two disciples who were "conversing and debating" as they walked along the road to Emmaus. "We were hoping that he would be the one to redeem Israel" (Luke 24:21). It is this very context of deep sharing between one disciple and another disciple that creates the context, the place, where the risen Jesus shows up. One of the most beautiful lines in the gospels is found here: "And it happened that while they were conversing and debating, Jesus himself drew near and walked with them." How beautiful is that! Even though they initially could not recognize him, Jesus was indeed there! Jesus himself even enters into the conversation and listens to them; he meets them where they are at. "What are you discussing as you walk along?"

The reason we have Christian community in our lives is not primarily to attend religious activities, not to share superficially and talk about the weather and sports. No, the reason we have community is to walk in discipleship with other disciples and share our human life and human faith, our light and our darkness, our joys and sorrows, with one another along the way. It is in this context that Jesus shows up, enters the room, and walks with us. Many times, the risen Christ is lost to us because we refuse to take the risk of entering into engaged, committed relationships with our brothers and sisters on the journey of faith.

Because we are broken

A primary reason we come together as a community of faith is because we are broken and need a savior. If we do not need a savior, why come? It is our broken parts that most cry out to God, and it is when we allow this cry to God to happen in the midst of the gathering of faith that we are in the best place to meet the saving love of God in Jesus. The disciples on the road to Emmaus were in deep pain over the death of Jesus, and that must have been the topic of their conversation. Jesus died in the worst possible way, upon a cross. They knew the words of Deuteronomy, "Cursed be the one who dies on a tree." All their hopes and dreams and spiritual meaning in Jesus up to that point were now dashed, and they walked in the deep darkness of no-faith.

It is this Christ, who was crucified in weakness and failure, that invites us to join one another in our weakness and failure to meet him. This says to us that we need not fear our weakness and brokenness; in fact, this is the very dimension of our humanity that most unites us in community. In Christian community we do not gather primarily in our success, achievements, and our personal and professional power; we gather in our weakness and brokenness before the cross of a suffering crucified savior. This experience and acceptance of our broken humanity is the beginning of Christian community and the beginning of the joy brought by the Lord. "O happy fault that earned so great, so glorious a Redeemer." This is the remarkable countercultural prayer we pray in our celebration of the Easter Vigil.

A shared brokenness

Let me illustrate brokenness through some contemporary examples.

When I was studying in the seminary, a priest offered a workshop on spirituality. The priest began by saying that it is only when we know and accept our own brokenness that we are able to discover God in our lives. The priest then went on to tell the following story about himself. He presided each day at the early morning Mass in the parish where he was living for several years. The same group of people came to this Mass every day. One day after Mass, one of the Mass participants came up to him and asked him if he noticed that the woman who always sat in the first pew was no longer coming. The priest said he had not. The person told him that she was not coming because she had died.

The priest then said to us that this was a moment of stark insight for him. He realized he did not know her, and over many years he had never taken the time to get to know her. Even more profoundly he went on to say that he realized that he did not really care to know her; that he didn't even know her name. The priest went to say that, at that moment, "I saw the depths of my own hypocrisy."

Hearing this priest talk like that about himself had a profound effect on me. I had never heard anyone share so deeply and honestly about their own brokenness and how it was a turning point in their encounter with Christ and their own personal transformation. I sat there quite stunned. I then began to think of all the forms of hypocrisy in my own life. I realized that his sharing with us freed me to begin to see myself more clearly, fully, and honestly. It was a moment of grace for me.

Another example was given by Bishop Robert Morneau of Green Bay, Wisconsin. Bishop Morneau spoke about a fellow bishop, Archbishop Murphy, who had been diagnosed with an aggressive form of leukemia. Archbishop Murphy spent thirty-eight days in intensive care and everyone thought he would die. Remarkably, he recovered. He later gave a presentation to the priests of his diocese and talked about the experience. Archbishop Murphy said that he had received thousands of letters during his time in the hospital, but of them, two letters really sustained him. The two letters were from Sammy, who was ten years old, and Sally, who was nine.

Sammy wrote:

> Dear Archbishop,
>
> You are very sick. And you are probably going to die. But you are going to go to heaven. And I have heard that heaven is a very nice place. You are going to like it there.
>
> Love, Sammy

Sally wrote:

> Dear Archbishop,
>
> My name is Sally. I am 9 years old. I have already had 39 surgeries in my life. So just hang in there.
>
> P.S. I am writing this from home, not CCD class.

The archbishop said that he received over two thousand letters, but these two letters really sustained him, because both came from the heart and spoke their respective truths. Sammy spoke the truth—that we will die and there is a heaven that awaits us. Sally shared her suffering, and in doing so she joined her suffering with Archbishop Murphy's suffering.

These two letters encapsulate the essence of Christian community. Christian community is the gathering of imperfect human people who continually speak the truth of our Christian faith one to another and freely share our common failures, sufferings, and joys as well. Christian community happens when we walk together and share our failure and suffering and do so in our common faith in Jesus as risen Lord and Savior. When we do this, we live in the truth of who we are and in the truth of who God in Jesus is.

When we refuse this kind of shared life, our gathering as people of faith misses out on the transformative power of the risen Jesus among us. We limit our capacity to enter into the very heart of the paschal mystery of a God who has lived in our midst, died, and risen so that we might die to sin and begin to live a new life now, a life that will be for all eternity with the community of saints in Christ our risen Lord. This is eloquently expressed in the following words attributed to Blessed John Newman: "So much holiness is lost to the church because brothers and sisters refuse to share the contents of their hearts one with another."

We all know how difficult this kind of sharing is for us—how we fear intimacy and sharing our weakness. Have you ever known someone who could never admit to being wrong? What are that person's relationships like? Imagine being married to a person who can never admit to being wrong. What would that marriage be like and how would it suffer? I often say of marriage, "If you have to be right, you are wrong." "If one of you wins an argument, you lose." Marriage is about a relationship. It is not about being "right." Christian community is not essentially about being "right," it is about accepting our brokenness, sharing that brokenness, and coming together to our Savior.

God's love is the security that enables us to be insecure. If we know we are loved with unconditional divine love, a security in this love is created within us so that we have nothing to fear of becoming vulnerable to our own weakness and to the full truth of who we are. Jesus fully shared in our humanity and showed us that *fear is useless; what is needed is trust* (see Luke 8:50). Trusting in God's love is the foundation of our lives; it frees us from self-protection and self-promotion in order to feel better about ourselves. It is living in openness to divine love and in openness to fellow believers on the journey of faith that creates the context for vibrancy in our shared experience of the risen Lord and allows us to receive more and more deeply the coming of the Holy Spirit into our lives.

Real presence

The Catholic Church has seven sacraments and believes in the real presence of Jesus in the Eucharist. If you are Catholic, the bar is set quite high for you as far as your fellow believers are concerned. To put it directly, if Jesus is in the Eucharist, where is Jesus when the Eucharist is consumed? In *you*! *All of you*! Someone once said, a little tongue-in-cheek, "Why is it we have an easier time believing that Jesus is in the eucharistic bread than in one another? A person looks much more like Jesus than a piece of bread. Is it because the bread is easier to swallow?"

All Christians also have the bar raised high in our relationship with other Christians because of the words of Scripture itself. Paul says, "Do you not know that your body is a temple of the Holy Spirit?" (1 Corinthians 6:19). The body of every Christian is a sacred place where God dwells. This is driven home profoundly by the actions of Jesus at the Last Supper in John's gospel. Jesus washes the disciples' feet. This gospel is not only about how we are to imitate Jesus in our service to one another but also about how Jesus himself is found today in one another. This gospel story ends with these words: "Amen, Amen, I say to you, whoever receives the one I send receives me, and whoever receives me receives the one who sent me" (John 13:20). May we so receive Jesus in one another, gathered together in him.

A gift of the Holy Spirit

Finally, community is a gift of the Holy Spirit—a consequence of the breath and fire of the Holy Spirit coming into our lives. It is only in the gift of the power of God's love given in the Holy Spirit that community will happen in our midst. In *Behold the Beauty of the Lord*, Henri Nouwen says this of community:

> Community is first and foremost a gift of the Holy Spirit, not built upon mutual compatibility, shared affection, or common interests but upon having received the same divine breath, having been given a heart set aflame by the same divine fire, and having been embraced by the same divine love.

In other words, community is part of the revolution.

PERSONAL REFLECTION

What do you think, and how do you feel, about Christian community as a sharing of our struggles, suffering, and joys with one another in faith?

Have you ever experienced this kind of sharing in faith with another person? What did this reveal to you?

CHAPTER FOURTEEN

MISSION

No one in the Bible is ever given an experience of God
without being, as a result, sent on a mission.

BISHOP ROBERT BARRON

A shared mission

While the heart of a vibrant and fervent faith community is the
sharing of life and faith, there remains another essential element
to fervent discipleship, and that is "mission." Without mission, a
Christian community becomes self-focused and ultimately dysfunctional. The dynamic is the same within marriage. When a
married couple focuses their lives solely on one another and
looks to this "one other" to fulfill all their needs and wants in life,
the marriage becomes insular and the growth of both individuals
is impeded. A healthy marriage is not two people living their lives
looking into each other's eyes and making this one other the sole
reason and focus of their life. A healthy marriage, and especially a
healthy Christian marriage, is two fully committed partners who
are standing side-by-side and looking in the same direction. That

direction is the values and mission of their life as a couple. This may create a new self-consciousness for many of us married folks. That we come together for a mission, a mission that our life as a couple is meant to empower and make possible.

It is a little-known fact for most couples marrying in the Catholic Church that this is an essential understanding of the nature of matrimony itself. The *Catechism of the Catholic Church* says this about Holy Orders *and* Matrimony: "Holy Orders and Matrimony are *directed towards the salvation of others*; if they contribute as well to personal salvation, it is through *service to others* that they do so. They confer a particular *mission* in the church and serve to build up the People of God" (1534, emphasis added).

How many couples who stand at the altar to receive the sacrament of matrimony have as the purpose for their marriage a calling to a "mission directed towards the salvation of others"? If married couples do not have this understanding, then it would be fair to say that most of the people who gather in church do not as well. In the Catholic Church, most lay people have simply never understood, and often never been told, of their baptismal and matrimonial call to mission. Therefore, whatever understanding of mission a Catholic might have they naturally abdicated to someone else, the clergy. This is at the heart of the reason why community as mission and the fervency that comes from a community on a mission is so lacking in our church today. This abdication is best expressed by the term "clericalism" as understood by Pope Francis.

Clericalism

Clericalism is not a religious person thinking he is better than others and has all the answers and walks through life with an air of superiority. For the pope, clericalism is something much deeper than this and involves lay people as well as clergy. Pope Francis sees that the average Catholic has been formed in a particular self-understanding. It is to think of themselves as just not that "religious" and that mission and holiness are essentially not their job but are for priests and nuns.

It is also a very capitalistic view of Christianity, since underneath there is a sense that we pay people to do this for us. Clericalism is nothing but the appropriation of what is proper to the baptized by the clerical caste. If, by virtue of their baptism, all Catholics are called to holiness and mission, to the task of witnessing to Christ, to evangelizing, to maturity—in short, to being missionary disciples—clericalism is ultimately a suppression of the baptismal identity. In this mindset, priests and nuns become the super-Christians who have the superpowers to do what ordinary Christians cannot.

This elevation leads to two outcomes: the isolation of the clergy and the immaturity of the baptized. St. Augustine said, "With you I am a Christian, for you I am a bishop." The Christian, no matter his or her ministry in the church, needs first to be a Christian *among* others, and, only then, *for* others. This expresses how the nature of healthy vibrant Christian community begins with the shared life and naturally flows into a shared mission. Clericalism simply would not exist if the first dimension of Christian community, that of a personal and deep sharing of life and faith, was a lived experience among us who gather as "church."

All of us baptized are first and foremost brothers and sisters together on this journey of faith, called to share our life and faith with one another. In this context, healthy ministry and mission happen. People are called forth to serve in their particular charism and gifts. A shared mission of all the baptized is the very lifeblood of the church and the very reason for the church's existence. Too many baptized and churchgoing Christians primarily see their life of faith as a personal journey to help them grow to be better people and get into heaven. The gospel makes it very clear that Jesus did not send the Holy Spirit just for you and me and our personal lives alone.

Mission in the Bible

In the gospels, we discover that immediately upon receiving the Holy Spirit the disciples were sent on a mission. So intimately united is the receiving of the Holy Spirit and the sending on mission that it appears as one and the same action of God. "Jesus came and stood in their midst and said to them, 'Peace be with you…As the Father has sent me, so I send you.' And when he had said this, he breathed on them and said to them, 'Receive the Holy Spirit'" (John 20:19–22). This was reiterated clearly on the day of ascension: "You will receive power when the Holy Spirit comes upon you, and you will be my witnesses in Jerusalem, throughout Judea and Samaria, and to the ends of the earth" (Acts 1:8). The Holy Spirit comes to bring power and make witnesses; witnesses who are sent on a mission to witness!

Another extraordinary fact revealed in this gospel is often overlooked: Jesus sends disciples who have just failed him in a significant fashion. In fact, Jesus does not even mention their personal and communal failure; Jesus just sends them! It almost appears that Jesus does not even see their failure. When he looks at them, he only sees their potential, their future as missionary disciples. That is how the risen Jesus looks at us! There is no one excused from the call to mission! This is important for all of us to remember—especially those who think mission does not apply to them because of their many personal failures.

We also see in the Bible what happens when someone has dismissed mission from their life of faith. "At the turn of the year when kings go out on campaign, David sent out Joab along with his officers and the army of Israel. David, however, remained in Jerusalem" (2 Samuel 11:1). Hidden in this seemingly simple statement is the fact that David, the great fighter and warrior king, stayed home and did not go out on mission. David abstained from the fight. What follows in the very next line is David's first glimpse of Bathsheba, the beginning of his destructive affair with her. The Bible is telling us not to shrink from our call to mission. It is mission itself that forms us as fervent disciples and sharpens our understanding of our personal calling to serve Christ.

Mission is faith

The gift of faith itself was not given to each of us for ourselves alone. In faith, we have received the love of God that now lives within us. The very nature of this divine love living within us moves us beyond ourselves to love of the other. Divine love is always self-giving and always in movement toward the other. As I said earlier, love in the gospel is two sides of the same coin, two dimensions of the same reality. If we genuinely receive the love of God, it would become the most natural impulse to give this love away to another.

Christian mission does not come as a command or law from an external source beyond ourselves; it comes as a natural impulse from within. There is no guilt or pressure from outside to mission, but true Christian mission comes as a response of joy from within. When one finds the pearl of great price, or the great treasure buried in the field, he or she sells all they have, out of *joy*, to obtain it. Everything is freely given out of joy to fully receive the pearl of great price, Jesus. We then discover that in the giving of our faith, our service, and love of others we receive more faith and more of the love of God, more of the pearl of great price, Jesus. This is why mission is so natural and essential to the life of a fervent disciple. It is not only natural; it is imperative. Our mission is nothing less than to be bearers of God's love and mercy to a world desperately in need of the saving love of God in Jesus Christ.

In other words, mission is part of the revolution. This "revolution of grace" occurs when people encounter the risen Jesus and grow into fervent disciples through prayer, service, community, and mission. Fervent disciples become revolutionaries of this revolution.

PERSONAL REFLECTION

Reflect on God's call to mission in your life.
Where have you seen this in your life?

Where do you see this call in your life now?

CONCLUSION

The fire of our faith

This book has been about building a fire, the fire of faith. This fire is ignited by personally encountering Jesus and is sustained and grows in its intensity by strategically incorporating prayer, service, community, and mission as central commitments in our lives. Ultimately, it is our choices that determine our discipleship, and it may help us to recall the words of Paul to Timothy:

> I remind you to stir into flame the gift of God that you have though the imposition of my hands. For God did not give us a spirit of cowardice but rather of power and love and self-control. 2 TIMOTHY 1:6–7

Essentially Paul is saying that it is our job to stay fired in our faith. To continually place the elements in our life that stoke the flames of the fire of divine love. It is our job, and much depends on our doing so, not only for ourselves but for all of humanity. If not now, when? If not us, who?

To find out more about becoming a fervent disciple go to
EncounteringJesusToday.org